Art & Memory in the churchyard

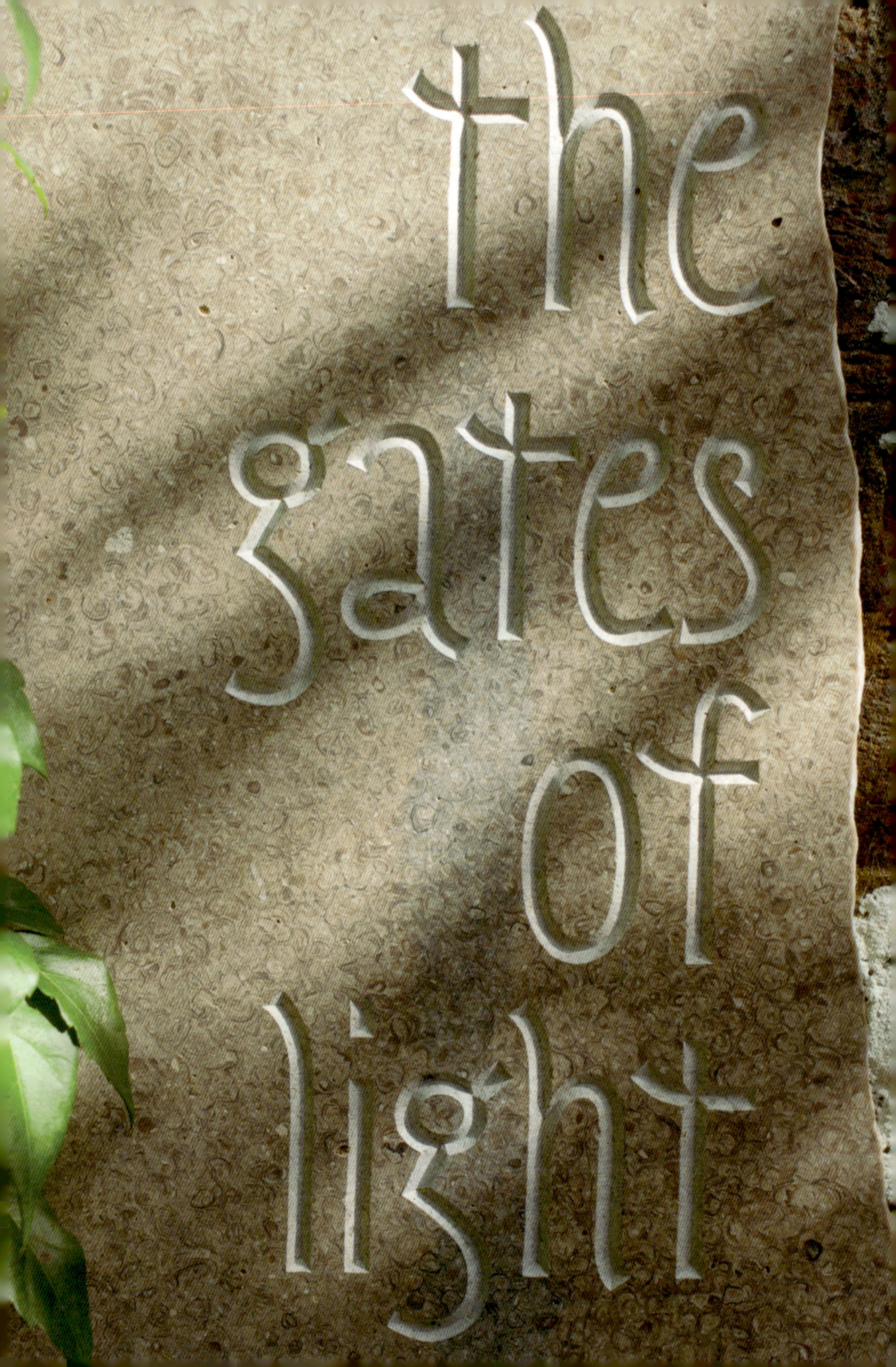
the
gates
of
light

ART & MEMORY IN THE CHURCHYARD

Edited by Christine Oestreicher

Foreword by Libby Purves

The Memorial Arts Charity 2010

ISBN 978 0 9515711 6 3

Published to coincide with the exhibition at
St Mary the Virgin, North Stoke, Amberley,
West Sussex BN18 9LS, 29 May–31 October 2010

Published by The Memorial Arts Charity
Snape Priory, Saxmundham
Suffolk IP17 1SA
T +44 (0)1728 688 393
Registered Charity No.1071427
www.memorialartscharity.org.uk
www.memorialsbyartists.co.uk

Cover: *Standing Stone: Touch* by James Salisbury,
2009, for the Art & Memory Collection (now at
Monnow Valley Arts Centre).
Preceding page: *Gates of Heaven* by Incisive
Letterwork, 2003, for the Art & Memory
Collection (now at Blair Castle, Perthshire).
Photos: Phil Baines & Kate Lyons

Contents

Dedicated to Dolf Mootham

FOREWORD Libby Purves

A gravestone, memorial to love, belongs both to the past and to the future. A stone in a churchyard is a landmark, given by private grief to the parish landscape in an odd and bittersweet kind of sharing. And, as years and centuries go by, we the first mourners will fade and the stones still stand as tribute and evidence of human love and respect.

So it is a delicate business, this placing of a private stone in a public place. The clergy to whom the churchyards are entrusted for the long future hold a high responsibility of one kind – historical, aesthetic, theological – while the mourners hold another kind of responsibility: to remember their dead as they were, individual personalities not ciphers or statistics. The artists who help the bereaved towards a right memorial hold a third responsibility: to their own craft and vision.

Sometimes these duties seem to clash. In the first intensely personal grief, none of us want to give any ground at all to anything impersonal or regulatory: it maddens us. At the same time, there has often been clerical anxiety or bewilderment about a mass of imprecise regulation, and a difficulty in reconciling stern traditional aesthetics with the wishes of surviving relatives, especially when the dead are very young. An image, a line, a dashing style which expresses a life as well as a loss, may fall foul of this anxiety for no good reason.

Taking a long view, though, there is less need for these conflicts than one might think. Look round the inscriptions in any churchyard with a deep history and you see how the spirit of each age has been interpreted in its stony memories – playful or devout, pragmatic or idealistic, tearfully doubtful or radiant with hope. People have always raised memorials, and the Church accepted them with only the mildest of restraints for many centuries.

But our mechanized age brought new troubles to the graveyards. A monotonous machine-cut ugliness has flooded in, from an industry well accustomed to embracing regulatory blandness: so today we reach a situation where – ironically – that very monotony is sometimes more acceptable to incumbents than a more imaginative personal bequest devised by thoughtful mourners and their collaborator artists.

Yet how will our far descendants judge us? What will they seek as they, like us today, wander among past memorials trying to understand the emotional truths of life and death? It is not our timid blandness which will feed them but art and sincerity: tributes which are individual as well as timeless. A renewal of courage and a broadening of sympathies would in many dioceses serve the future, as well as the past, better than it sometimes does today.

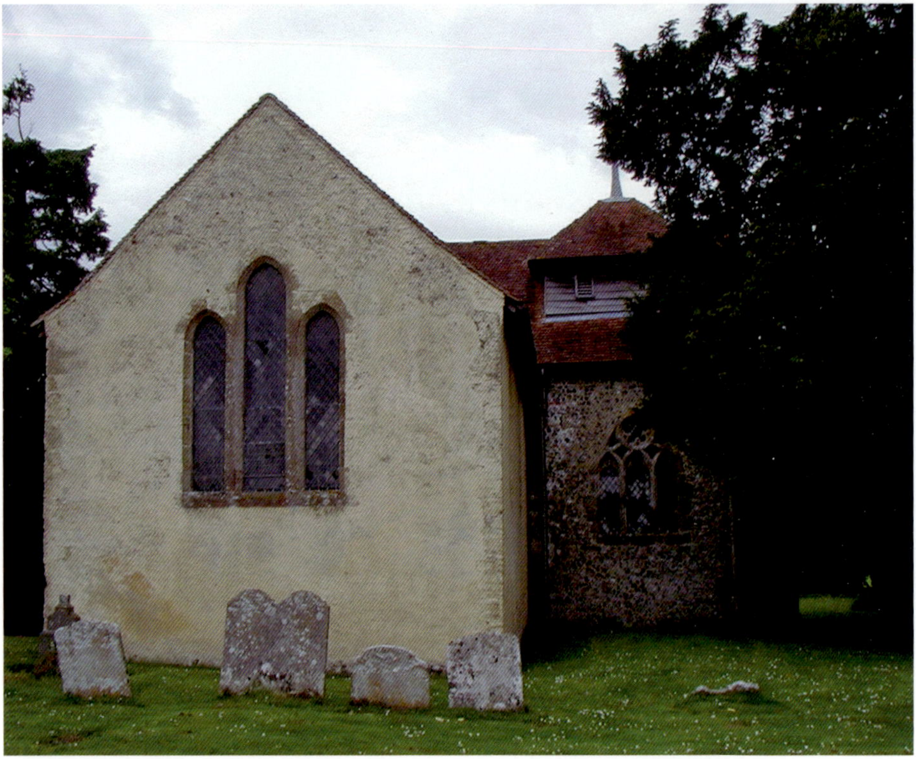

THE ART & MEMORY EXHIBITION AT ST MARY'S, NORTH STOKE

Janet Aidin

It was through the lettercutter Richard Kindersley that I first came to hear about the work of Harriet Frazer, Memorials by Artists and The Memorial Arts Charity. Richard had done work for us, so in 2004 it was natural to ask him to carve a memorial stone for my parents. The beautiful result is in Wiggonholt Churchyard. In the meantime I had helped to set up a Friends Group for my former parish church at North Stoke which had passed into the care of the Churches Conservation Trust. I visited the Art & Memory exhibition at West Dean in 2009 several times. I was quite unprepared for its scope. It dawned on me that the churchyard at North Stoke would make an ideal setting for the work of the Charity. With the support of the Trust and the Friends Committee I approached Harriet, and the result can now be seen.

The Church of St Mary the Virgin, North Stoke, sits high on the South Downs and is a place of special beauty and history. Although the Church was vested in the Churches Conservation Trust in 1992, the churchyard belongs to Amberley Parish. The Church is redundant but is still consecrated, as is the churchyard. Ashes are occasionally interred, but burials have long fallen into abeyance, so the churchyard is uniquely able to accept and absorb a temporary exhibition of this kind.

We have a fine tradition of letter-carving and memorial art in England, going back for hundreds of years. Visiting churchyards and reading tombstones is an honoured tradition in this country. Tombstones not only tell us who died, but how their memory was recorded and sustained in earlier times. Some are simple folk art; others are masterpieces of sophisticated carving and expression in a variety of materials. None is futile, none perfunctory. In each we sense that someone has striven for the best.

Anyone who has taken a brass rubbing will have experienced the thrill of owning a piece of memorial art – at least in replica. But when it comes to remembering our own dead the choice is rather more confusing. Fine memorials can be found, but often the bereaved have no idea how to go about it and cannot, somehow, focus on what they truly want. I have spoken to so many people who felt that the memorial they chose was not what they had wanted in their heart of hearts. It did not live up to their idea, and even seemed a little impersonal. They had not been aware of what was possible, or that decisions needed time of their own. So they settled for less than they had hoped.

There is also the problem of what is acceptable to the church authorities. Gravestones in English churchyards are controlled by the regulations of the local Diocesan Chancellor. Regulation seeks to promote acceptable types of memorial stone and prevent what is unsuitable by a degree of standardisation. As a result, beautiful memorials which could have enhanced the churchyard are often excluded, while drab and poorly-designed work is permitted. On a recent visit to a breathtaking mediaeval churchyard in the Welsh Marches, I found standardisation taken to an extreme: the older graves were of local stone, randomly set, but the 20th century graves were marked without exception by orchestrated ranks of polished granite, a crushing 'solution' indeed.

With all these ideas in mind, the Memorial Arts Charity and the Friends of St Mary the Virgin, North Stoke, have mounted an exhibition of contemporary memorials. The exhibition has been made possible with the permission and support of both the Parochial Church Council of Amberley and the Churches Conservation Trust. The aim is to enhance the quality of memorials in general and to widen the scope of what is permitted in churchyards by showing gifted and inspiring examples of work. We hope the display will stimulate public interest so that people can learn more about memorials and consider what is possible before the need arises. Above all, it will allow the interested public to see what skilled design and craftsmanship can achieve. It is hoped this exhibition will also raise questions and engender debate. In this way the private art of memory becomes available to all.

Janet Aidin, Secretary of The Friends of St Mary the Virgin, North Stoke

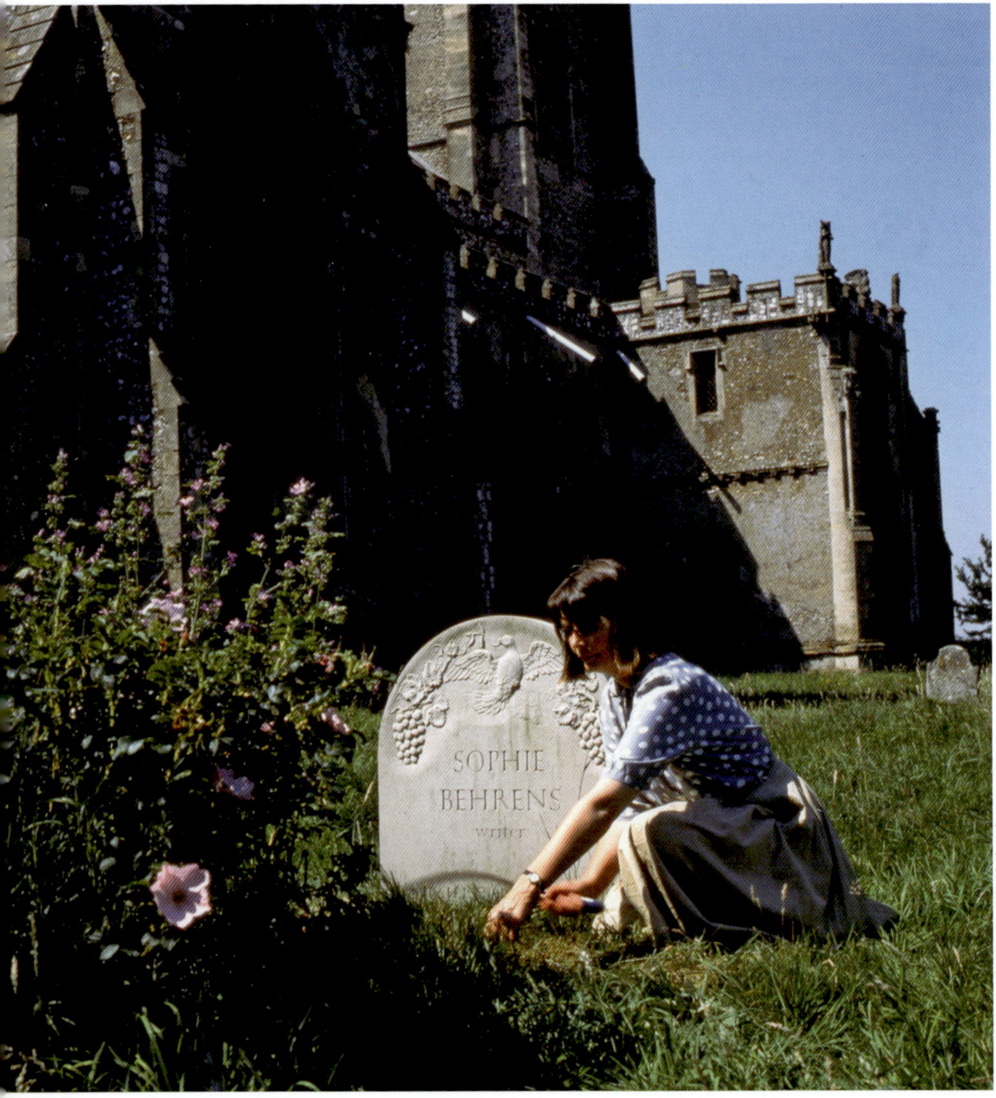

Simon Verity (the Verity Workshop)

INTRODUCTION Harriet Frazer

We are extremely grateful to The Friends of St Mary the Virgin, The Churches Conservation Trust and Amberley PCC for this unexpected opportunity to hold an exhibition in such a beautiful, and completely unspoilt, consecrated churchyard.

All the works shown were commissioned by The Memorial Arts Charity to found The Art & Memory Collection. The makers were asked to design something they felt inspired to create on a memorial theme. Nine of these works were first shown at The Art of Remembering exhibition in the gardens of Blickling Hall, Norfolk in 1998. The rest were commissioned in 2008 and shown for the first time at West Dean Gardens in 2009.

I founded Memorials by Artists in 1988 to help people overcome the hurdles that can arise when ordering a memorial. The idea stemmed from our ignorance as a family, 25 years ago, of how to set about having a headstone made for my 26 year old step-daughter, Sophie Behrens. We did not know how to begin, let alone how much would be involved in having a unique and beautiful stone made for Sophie.

Through an extraordinary series of chance connections I discovered the work of Simon Verity. Sitting in his kitchen two years after Sophie died and talking over who she was and our ideas for her stone was such a relief. He understood what we were trying to convey, he could answer all our questions and his work was beautiful.

At the time our family had not understood that there are strict rules and regulations for churchyard memorials and we had thought that Sophie's plot was ours, since we had paid for it. When I showed the design to the vicar, simply thinking he would be interested and delighted to have this beautiful memorial in his churchyard, he said alas, we would not be allowed the four lines from one of Sophie's poems (she was already a published writer). He then showed me the diocescan rules and regulations for churchyard memorials. These said that:

> Inscriptions should be simple, dignified and reverent. Passing sentiments are to be avoided. Encouraged are brief epitaphs with biblical or well-known hymnal words which reflect the life and work of the deceased.

I was not made aware of the faculty procedure (ecclesiastical planning permission).

The design was adapted – no epitaph now, simply the word WRITER.

Two people wrote to me after seeing a photograph of Sophie's memorial in the newspaper, both saying the same thing – that they had seen her headstone in a remote country churchyard and 'wondered who she was'.

Not everything should have to be easily understood and explainable. It is good to leave a sense of mystery, for the passer-by to stand still awhile and wonder who the person was and what the words and symbols mean.

Our hope is that people will be struck by the work shown and that one day the churchyard rules will be eased to allow for more creativity and freedom of expression.

THE WORK OF THE MEMORIAL ARTS CHARITY

Christine Oestreicher

The Memorial Arts Charity is the only national charity in the UK with the specific brief of fostering contemporary memorial art, its objects being 'to promote, for the public benefit, education in and appreciation of the arts and crafts associated with memorials, particularly good design and lettercarving.'

Founded by Harriet Frazer in 1998, the charity came into being at a time of neglect of the memorial arts and crafts and the skills that underpin them. Practical, high quality training had declined markedly in the post-war era and lettering was dropped as a subject in most art schools. Opportunities for serious grounding in the craft were therefore rare.

It was a time, also, when even more than nowadays, death, mortality and bereavement were subjects many people found difficult and shied away from. Indeed, during the years when Harriet and I were first searching for places to hold our permanent exhibition of works on memorial themes, the reaction we met was often one of nervousness about whether the public might be 'put off' by the word 'memorial'. The Memorial Arts Charity's exhibitions at Blickling Hall (1998) and West Dean (2009) proved overwhelmingly that there is, on the contrary, a great need for opportunities to engage with all aspects of this important subject. It was for this reason that we set out to establish a permanent and evolving collection of commemorative works by contemporary lettercarvers – works that would invite contemplation as well as informing people about lettercarving, a much neglected art form.

The collection – known as the *Art & Memory Collection* – finally came into being in 2009 and is being launched nationwide during 2010 and 2011 at six varied and beautiful sites across the UK.

Since its inception, in 1998, the Charity has directed its energies to addressing gaps in lettercarving training, running an apprenticeship scheme and lettercarving workshops throughout the UK, and engaging with trade monumental masons, the church and other organisations to influence standards and raise public awareness and appreciation of memorial arts relevant to the 21st century.

The Memorial Arts Charity has also increased employment opportunities for lettercarvers through its wholly owned trading company, Memorials by Artists which provides advice and assistance to people wanting to commission a memorial, particularly the recommending of appropriate artists and dealing with technical matters such as the legal requirements for churchyards and cemeteries.

In tandem with Memorials by Artists, we continue to work to encourage more creative rules and regulations for churchyards and cemeteries so that the art of lettercarving can continue to flourish. It is a welcome sign that, in 2005, we were approached by the Secretary of Canterbury Diocesan Advisory Committee (DAC), Ian Dodd, about the possibility of holding an 'exhibition of high quality memorials' at Canterbury. To quote from his letter of 22 November 2005 to Harriet Frazer, 'This was really in response to the run-of-the-mill applications received by the DAC for work which was probably acceptable, but really not of a standard which would enhance the building in which it was set.'; and, from his letter of 12 April 2006, '...inspiring people to realise that individuals can be commemorated in unusual and individual ways without the need to sacrifice high quality of design and execution.'. That these ideas coincided so perfectly with our own has culminated in Canterbury Cathedral Memorial Garden becoming one of the sites for the Art & Memory Collection, thanks to the encouragement of the Dean, the Very Revd Robert Willis; the Canon Treasurer, Dr Edward Condry; Ian Dodd, secretary to the Canterbury DAC, and Heather Newton, Head of Conservation. The other sites for the permanent collection are: Blair Castle, Perthshire; Monnow Valley Arts Centre, Herefordshire; Arnos Vale Cemetery, Bristol; Winterbourne House and Garden, Birmingham and Grimsthorpe Castle, Lincolnshire.

The invitation to show our work at North Stoke is another important and much appreciated sign that the Church, and people close to it, are listening – just as we are listening to them.

It is to be hoped that as time goes on the work of the Memorial Arts Charity, together with encouragement from the Church, will bring wider acceptance and new opportunities for lettercarvers, so that future generations will have the pleasure and fascination of coming across beautiful, intriguing memorials that reflect well on our times.

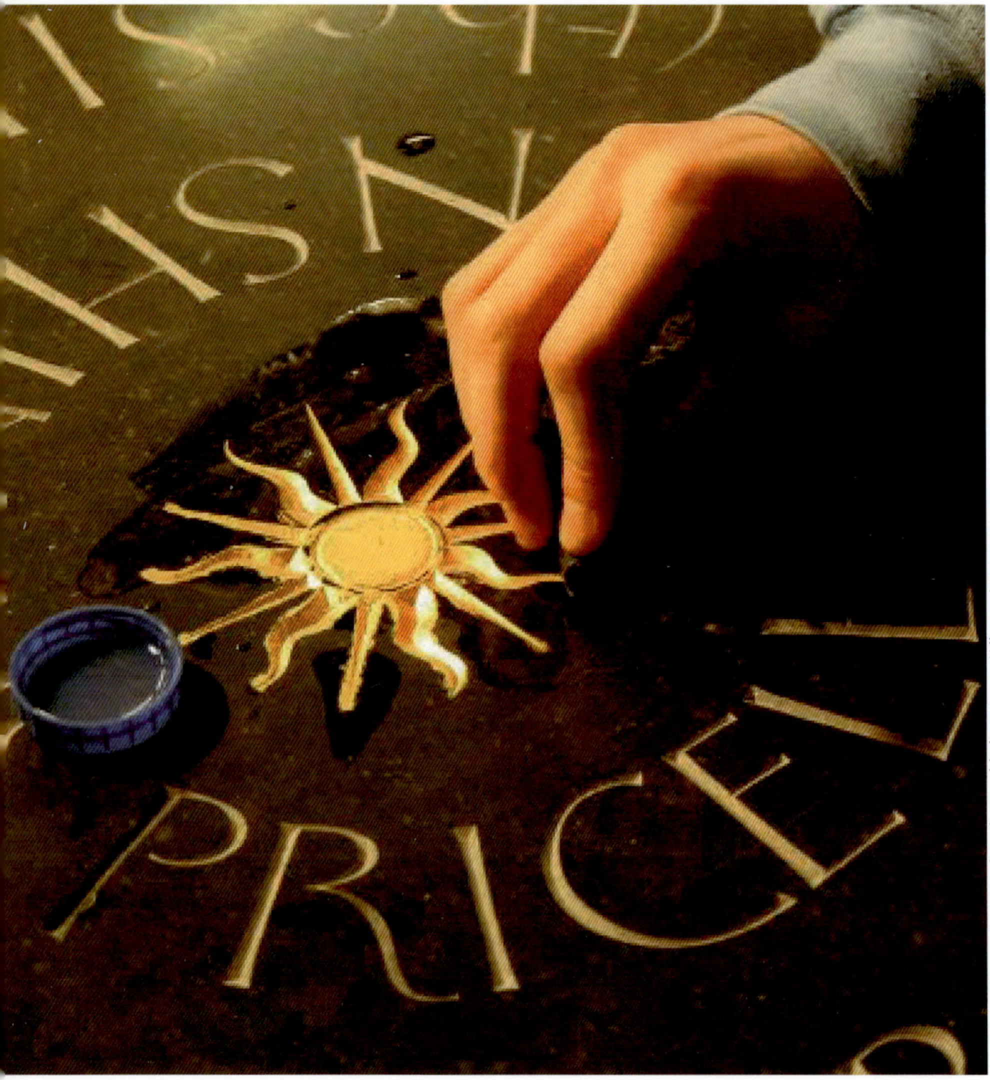

Apprentice Wayne Hart sanding down gilded carving in Kilkenny Limestone

THE ART & CRAFT OF LETTERCARVING

Lynne Alexander & Clare Austyn

The Memorial Arts Charity is an arts-based educational charity. Our work includes educational courses, apprenticeships and national exhibitions. Since 1998, when it was founded, the Charity has been successful in helping people from all walks of life to discover and appreciate the art and craft of lettercarving – an important aspect of the UK's cultural heritage going back hundreds of years.

For those people who are new to the subject of lettercarving, we hope a brief introduction will help explain what it involves. A lettercarver designs the letters and layout for inscriptions and then carves them. The letters may be designed afresh for each commission. The designing, spacing, layout and carving of the letters all require a high level of skill. The work of a lettercarver has traditionally included the making of memorials, large and small. Some lettercarvers shape and prepare the stone, or wood, themselves. Decorative motifs and embellishments may be carved in addition to the lettering. This combination of techniques, executed with the skill of a craftsman and the eye of an artist, produces highly individual pieces of work ranging from memorials to architectural lettering, public art and experimental personal work. Not all the work of a lettercarver is necessarily on a large scale, as lettercarving lends itself perfectly to small objects as well. Experienced lettercarvers sometimes work in other materials such as metal and glass.

It was ten years ago that the Memorial Arts Charity initiated a series of workshops to support the training of lettercarvers, and we now run an Apprenticeship Scheme and an annual nationwide series of short courses, thus sustaining the development of lettercarving for future generations. The workshops are tutored by some of the UK's finest lettercarvers. They all have successful careers in lettering and are also gifted and inspiring teachers, keen to share their knowledge and love of this craft with others.

In 2008 we raised funds for TOUCH workshops with visually impaired and blind children, tutored by Kevin Carey, Chairman of the RNIB, to coincide with the 2009 launch exhibition of The Art & Memory Collection at West Dean Gardens. The Charity also organised two lettering workshops in a local school. We will be developing both series of workshops further in the future.

In 2010 we will be launching The Friends of the Memorial Arts Charity with a new annual journal – *Touchstone*. Lettercarving has strong visual appeal and we will be making more of this over the coming years, initially in the form of a limited edition calendar and postcards. We are passionate about helping this craft to continue to flourish.

The best way to keep up to date with our work and progress is to visit our website www.memorialartscharity.co.uk

GOOD DESIGN Nicholas Sloan

We talk a lot about the importance of commissioning well-designed memorials, but what exactly do we mean by this? How can we tell whether a design is good or not?

The least one should be able to expect is that a stone is considered carefully, bearing the person commemorated in mind: what would they have liked? How do we reflect in the design their personality and the nature of our relationship with them? If this process is undertaken with a sympathetic artist, someone to whom the material, the words and the lettering form a mutually dependent whole, then whatever results should, in the widest sense, be good. The quality of the design will emerge from the artist's skill and love of making, inspired by their impression of the deceased.

In contrast to this however, churchyards are filling up with commercial stones which are largely mass-produced, with the lettering cut by machine or sandblasted, often it seems with minimal attention to design. This trend is having a decidedly detrimental effect on the cultural richness of churchyards. Furthermore, such memorials can never have the same sense of life and rightness as a stone which has been discussed and evolved with the artist who is going to make it.

Happily, there are many sympathetic artists to call on. The Bayly slate by John Nash (p.27) is a fine example of excellence in design and cutting in the mainstream of the English tradition. Michael Rust's memorials to John Donne (p.29) are similarly traditional, laid out with poise and cut with great delicacy. It is particularly interesting to see oak presented alongside stone, similar in design and yet so different in feel.

Both of these stones, as with several of the others (the meditation marker by Andrew Daish [p.20], the *Bless* standing stone by Una Sullivan [p.33], the slate to Aileen Sloan [p.31]) are conspicuous in being tall in proportion to their width and yet not particularly large in overall size. Many lettercutters resist the modern tendency towards squat commercial stones, but this can create problems with the regulations, where maximum heights and minimum widths are often specified, without reference to overall area.

The slate by John Das Gupta to his father (p.21) is also narrow in proportion, though in this case rather large as well. Such an intensely considered and imaginative synthesis of Welsh slate and Bengali imagery and words would be a wonderful thing to come across in an English churchyard, but the regulations current in many dioceses might proscribe this stone, not only on account of its size, but for its wording and imagery as well.

Churchyards are of course very special places and clearly there have to be some limits as to what is allowed in them, but increasingly I feel that what matters most in maintaining the beauty of churchyards is limiting drabness and encouraging care in design and the quality of making. Discouraging the unusual is by contrast completely counterproductive. The issue is not so much one of taste as of thoughtfulness: given sufficient thought and skill, I believe that beauty can usually be left to look after itself.

Although they are made by different people in different materials, there is something of a family likeness between Bettina Furnée's 'C'est dur de mourir...' (p.24) and Robyn Golden Hann's 'Blessed are they that mourn...' (p.25). Like many of the stones in this exhibition, they are not memorials to individuals, and so there can be no sense of their being tailored to the specific character of a real person, but it does not follow that the design is arbitrary: both have been thoughtfully made to convey a sense of sympathetic sadness, through the irregular artlessness of the shapes, the softened edges and the very evidently hand-cut lettering. The rougher of the three stones to Aileen Sloan ('Thanks Mum', p.30) was also intended to suggest tenderness and intimacy, in contrast to the more formal slate (p.31).

All of the stones on exhibition illustrate the humanising effect of hand-cut lettering, and show how the nature of the lettering can affect the feel of the words; but carving too can have a powerful effect on a memorial. In Geoffrey Aldred's *Stone to the Homeless* (p.18), the lettering is subsidiary to the original design with its sheltered figure, while Harry Brockway's shepherd (p.19) makes a wonderfully protective graphic statement over whatever inscription might appear below. The representation of Ben Shahn's 'chop' is integral to the design (p.26) and illustrates how a graphic device can be used in balance with the other elements to create the integrated whole which should be the aim of every well-designed memorial.

THE CATALOGUE: WORKS FROM THE ART & MEMORY COLLECTION

GEOFFREY ALDRED

Stone to the Homeless
Hopton Wood Stone
1220 x 610 x 102mm

The inspiration for this work was Yorkie Greaves, a seventy-four year old homeless man who died in Kentish Town, London, in 1996, having lived on a park bench for fifteen years. The spontaneous tributes by local people prompted me to design a memorial to all the homeless dead, many of whom die tragically young.

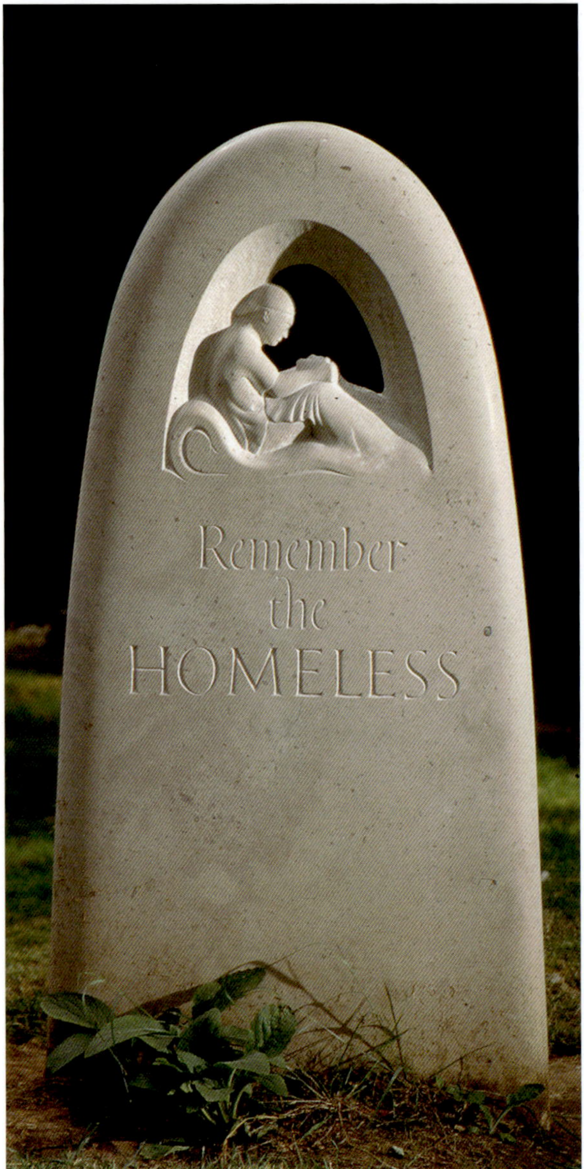

HARRY BROCKWAY

Headstone to a Shepherd
Portland Stone
1000 x 600 x 90mm

I was once commissioned to illustrate John Milton's poem, Lycidas. I thought the famous closing lines would be very suitable for a headstone. The image of the shepherd is one I have used several times in my work.

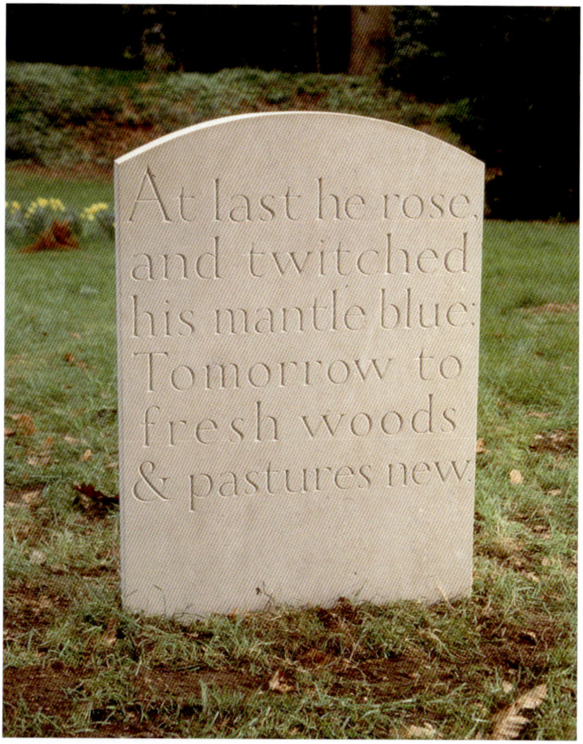

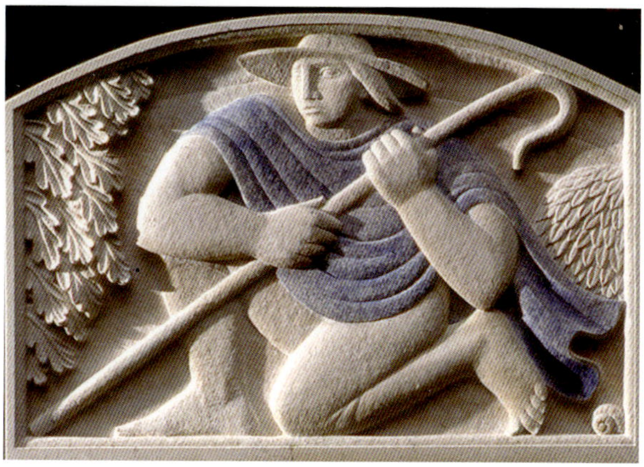

ANDREW DAISH

Meditation Marker
Welsh Slate
1220 x 280 x 32mm

I have learned from both personal experience and the experiences of bereaved clients that when you lose a much-loved person you suddenly become very aware of your own mortality and enter a state of reflection. We realise that our lives consist of contrasts – to understand joy we have to experience pain and to understand love we have to experience rejection. With these thoughts in mind, I decided to design a gravemarker that celebrated or 'blessed' four of the most obvious feelings we experience in life, feelings that make us both human and mortal.

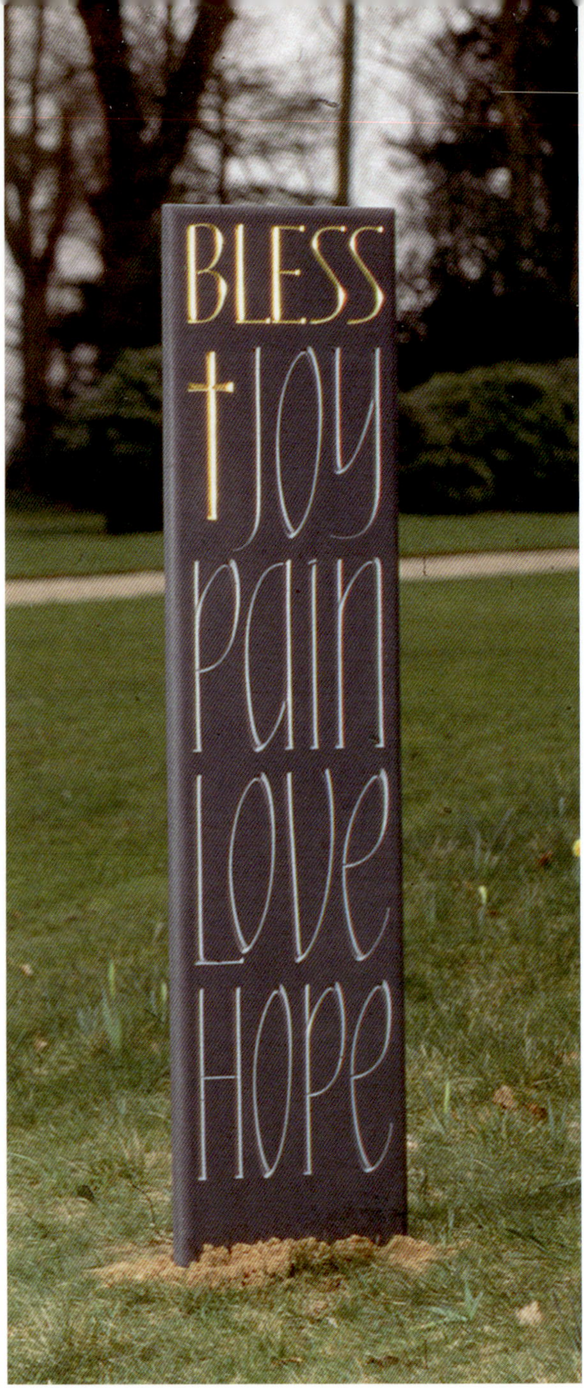

JOHN DAS GUPTA

Lantern Headstone
Welsh Slate
1525 x 510 x 51mm

This stone is to my father, a Bengali, who died in 1959 in Darjeeling and was cremated there in the customary manner. I felt the design should strongly reflect his Indian origins, yet take some account of the memorial traditions that exist here in the UK. The front of the stone arries the biographical facts and shows a lantern motif – an idea taken from a television programme about the kite-flying season in India. This season is traditionally ended with the release of a delicate paper lantern containing a tiny flame. It drifts precariously into the evening sky, a vulnerable yet potent beacon which seemingly captivates the crowd of onlookers by its strange aura of magic.

The reverse of the stone is a more complex arrangement of English and Bengali: short passages from poems by Rabindranath Tagore whose work is still loved throughout Bengal. These combined texts overlay an abstracted pattern, itself a play on image and ground, which covers the entire surface.

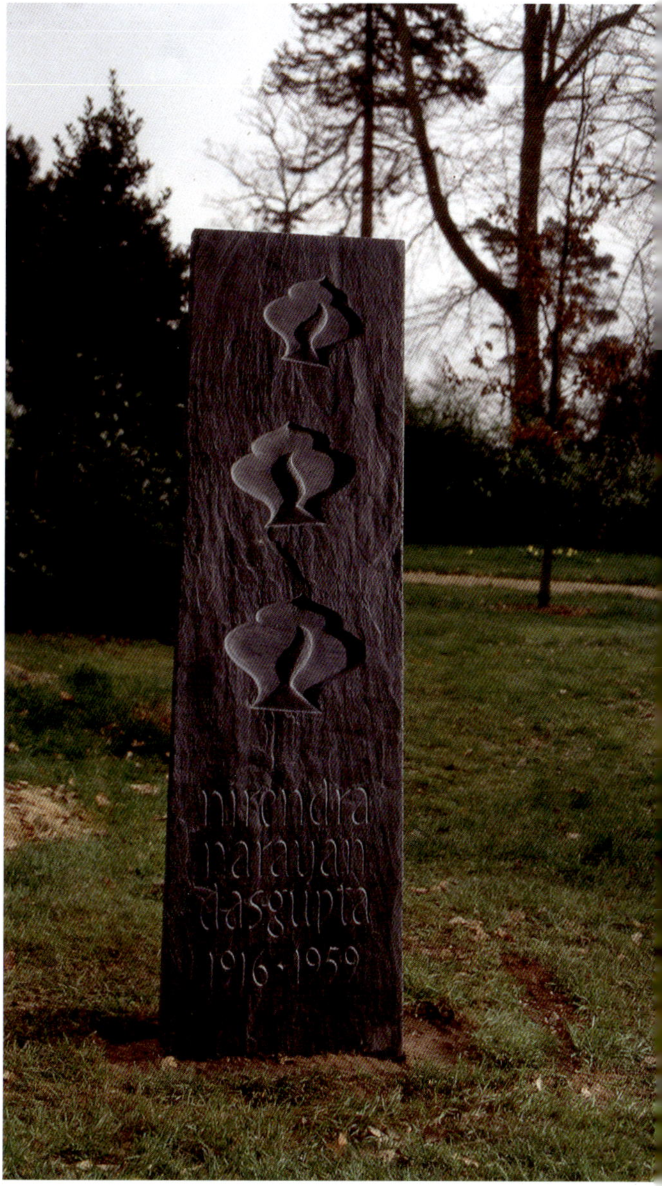

CHRIS ELSEY

I am the Light of the World
Natural Welsh Slate
monolith approx. 990 x 335 x 127mm, on large natural pebble

This piece reflects on Christ redeeming us by His suffering on the cross. Rock of Ages, the hymn by Augustus Toplady, was Michael Renton's favourite. Michael worked on many commissions for Memorials by Artists and we all miss him since he passed away in 2001. This piece is also in memory of Paul, my brother.

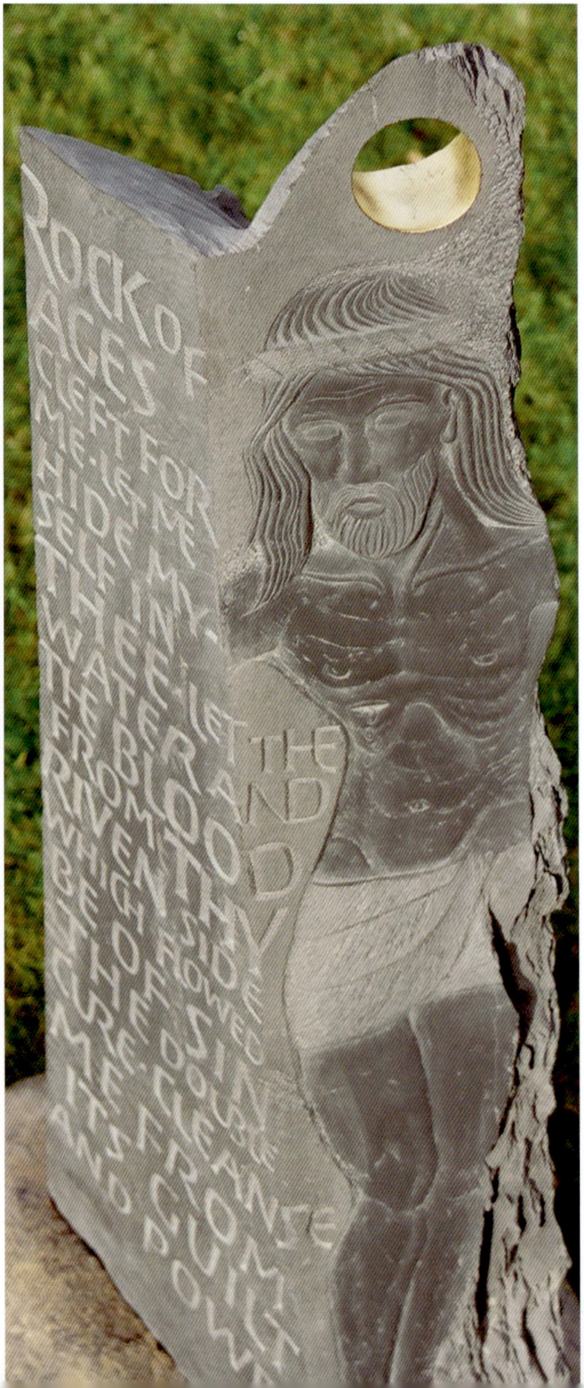

PETER FURLONGER

Leaves of the Trees
Cumbrian Green Slate
610 x 455 x 75mm

The idea for this design was derived from a recent commission. The frieze text was chosen by the family as an expression of their sense of the value of their young daughter's life. I have combined with this a text which, while expressing a sense of the impermanence of life, embodies an idea of continuity and joyful rebirth.

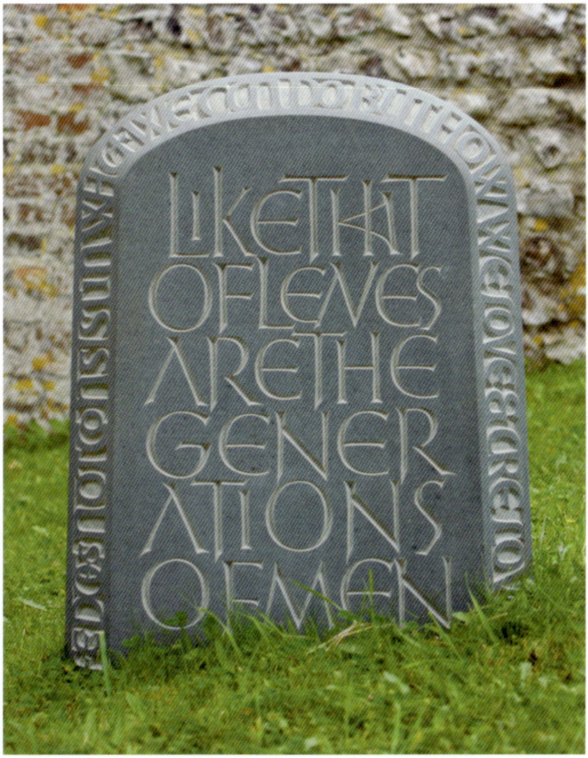

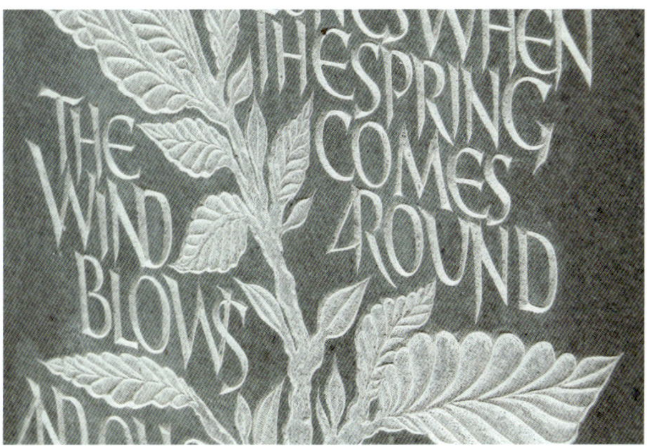

BETTINA FURNEE

Mourir au Printemps
Welsh Slate (two pieces)
610 x 455mm & 405 x 405mm

This pair of markers is conceived as a memorial to those who died too young. Maybe we grieve most painfully for a life lost before it could ever be fulfilled.

Words from the song, *Le Moribond* by Jacques Brel

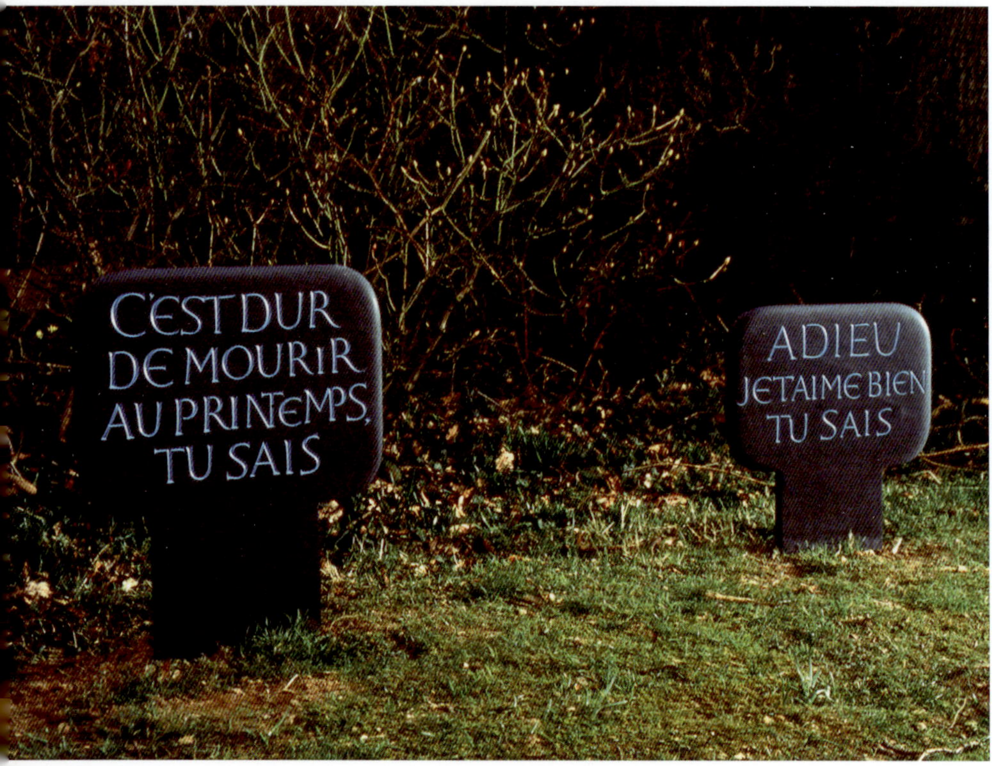

ROBYN GOLDEN-HANN

Portland Stone
900 x 590 x 75mm

Memorials fulfil our spiritual need to make a mark; to show that we were here. Letters, though nothing more than simple abstract shapes, convey complex ideas and expressions of humanity. Lettercarving is the alchemy through which the artist realises the magical power of letters and gives them meaning.

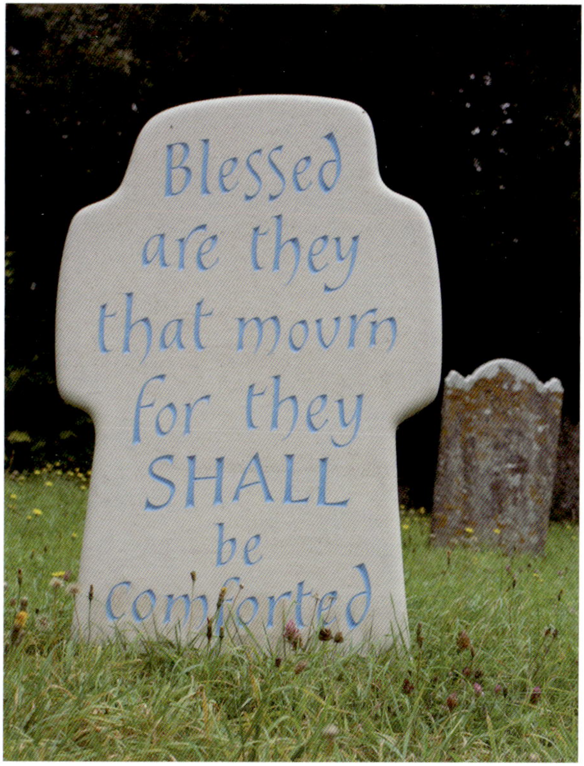

JOHN NASH

Memorial Tribute to Ben Shahn
Welsh Slate
815 x 30 x 38mm

Artists, writers and musicians often have headstones bearing appropriate objects and quotations, but all too seldom are these representations drawn from the artist's own work. Why shouldn't, for example, a composer have a bar of his own music on his tombstone? This exhibition piece shows, on one side, Shahn's 'chop' or identifying stamp composed of letters of the Hebrew alphabet, and on the other, an observation from one of his lectures which any artist or craftsman would do well to take to heart: 'Craft is that discipline which frees the spirit and style is the result'.

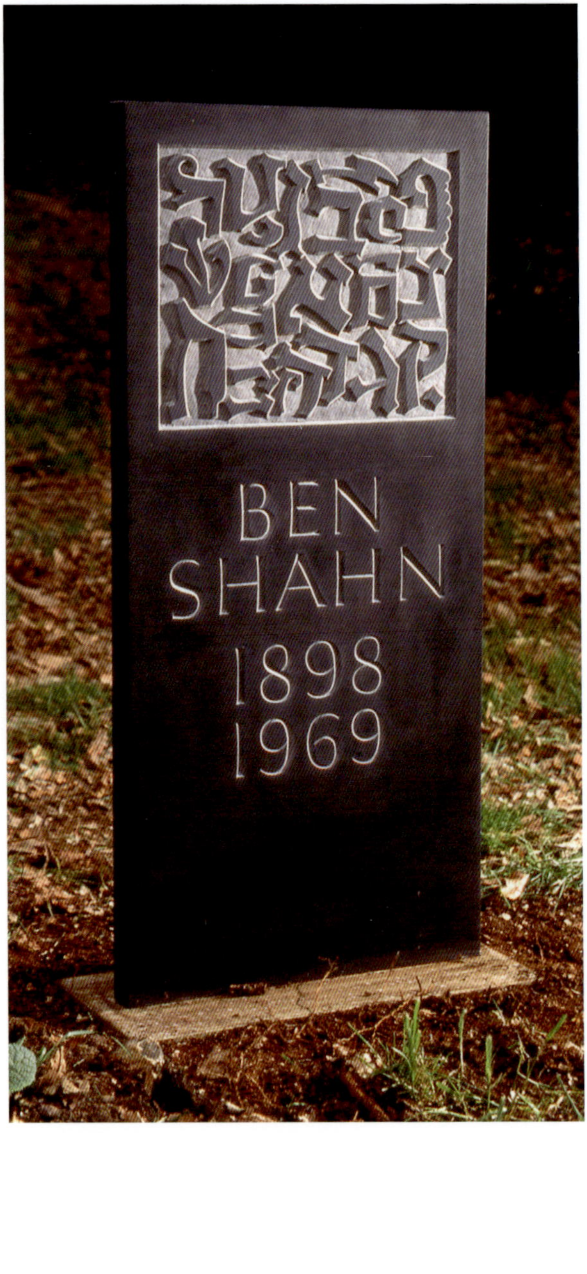

JOHN NASH

The original Memorial to John & Cicely Bayly
Welsh Slate
785 x 405 x 64mm

A replacement had to be made in 2008 when it was found that this stone, cut in 2002 for a Devon churchyard, had developed a hairline crack at the top.

Clare Twiss (née Bayly) has now kindly donated her parents' original memorial to the Art & Memory Collection

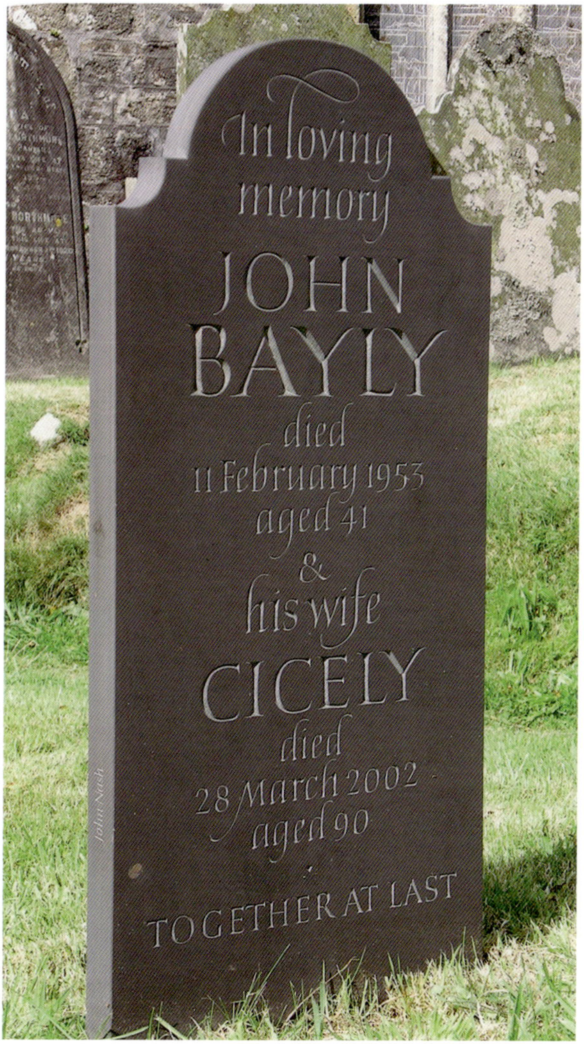

RON PARSONS

Memorial to William Green
Iroko hardwood
1065 x 535 x 75

I first met William Green in 1950 when I was a student at Exeter College of Art and he was the Principal. In 1962, when my work as a lettercutter and heraldic artist was beginning to become known, he gave me invaluable advice on the finer points of heraldry and design. He had a vast knowledge of many subjects including art, church architecture, classical music and gardening, all of which were made available to me just for the asking. It was in 1963 that I married his daughter Audrey. With all these happy memories in mind, I decided I must design a memorial to celebrate his life.

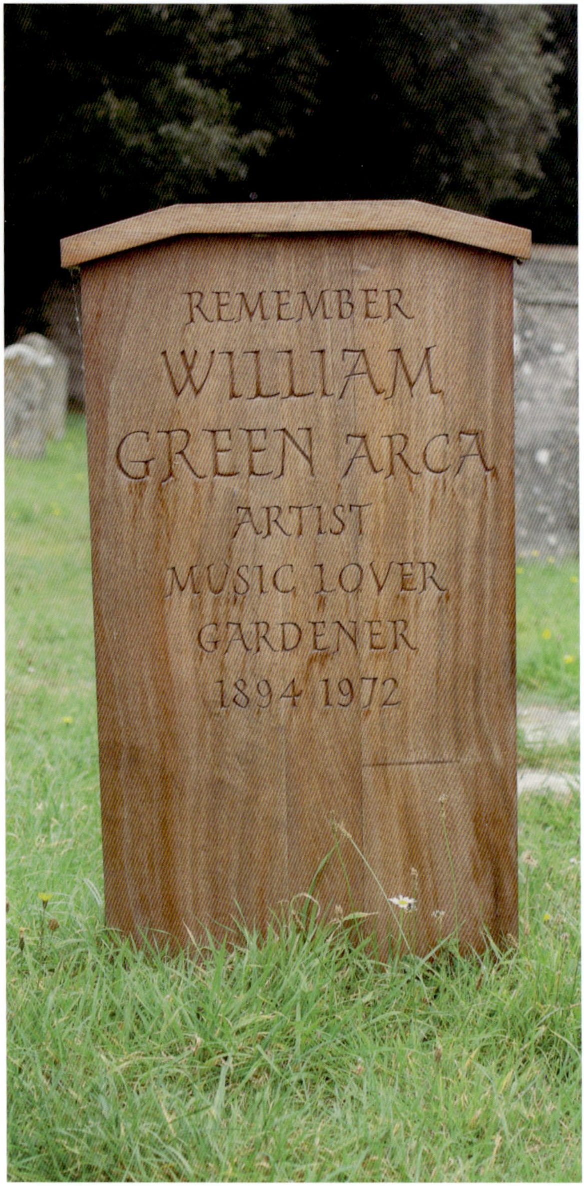

MICHAEL RUST

Memorial to John Donne
Nabresina Limestone
1200 x 500 x 75mm
English Oak
1200 x 500 x 75mm

Although these identical twin memorials, one in limestone, the other in oak are to a man long dead, his ideas and poems continue to speak to us all. You are invited to feel the material from which they are made, the one millions of years old with fossilised markings, the other less than 100 years old and warmly organic.

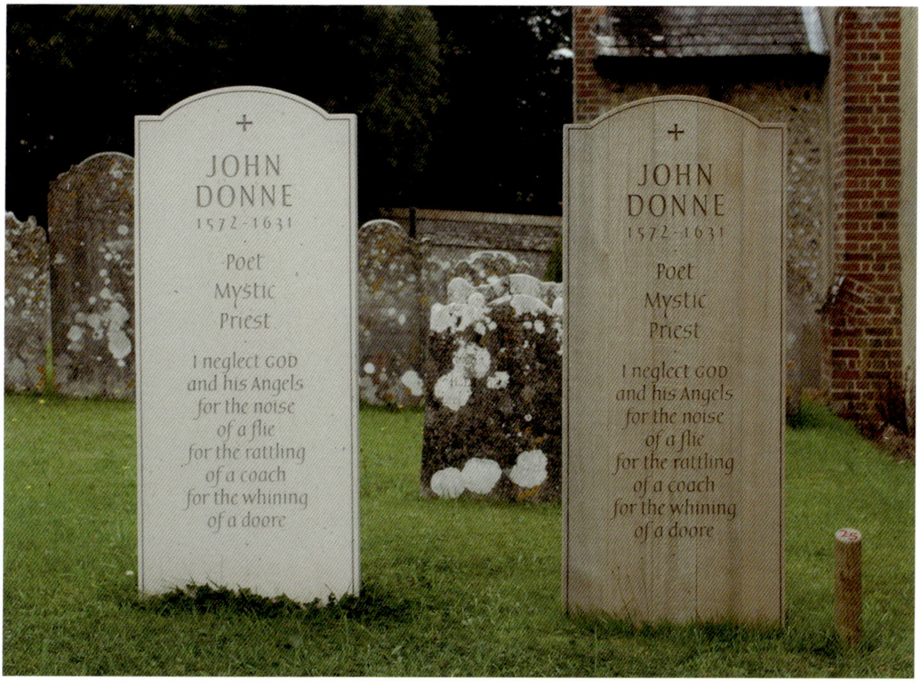

NICHOLAS SLOAN

(with ThomasonCudworth)

Three Aspects of Aileen Sloan
Cornish Slate 1130 x 430 x 41mm
Purbeck 915 x 585 x 125mm (average dimensions of rough and irregular stone)
Terracotta 915 x 510 x 100mm

The intention in making three different stones in memory of the same person was to show how variously someone can be represented, according to the nature of the design, the material, and the choice of wording. In other words: design makes a big difference to how we perceive the person through the stone.

The idea of commemorating my own mother came later. She does not have a grave, and I had never made a stone for her, but regretted this. It suddenly seemed to fall into place that each stone could represent an aspect of her character, so I started designing the three variations: a formal slate, a less formal design in rough Purbeck, and an almost wholly pictorial version reflecting my mother's interest in gardening and bee-keeping. At this point it occurred to me that the third 'stone' would be an ideal vehicle for the wonderful modelling of my friends Philip and Karin Thomason, and an opportunity to show the potential of their high-fired terracotta as a practical material for memorials.

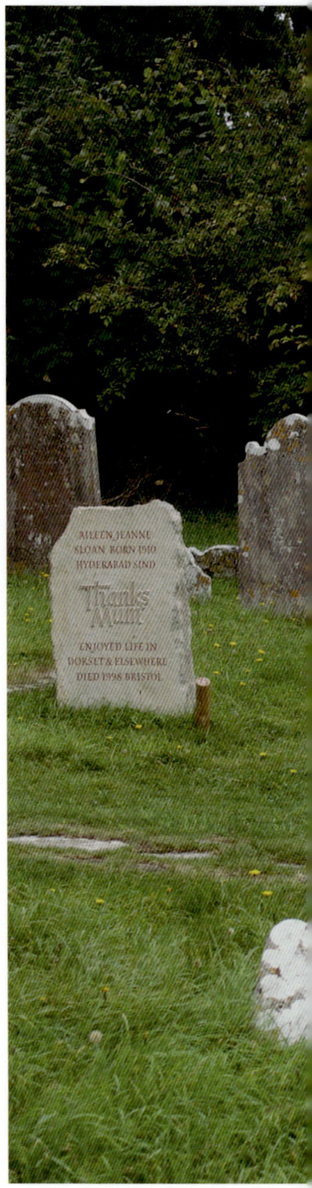

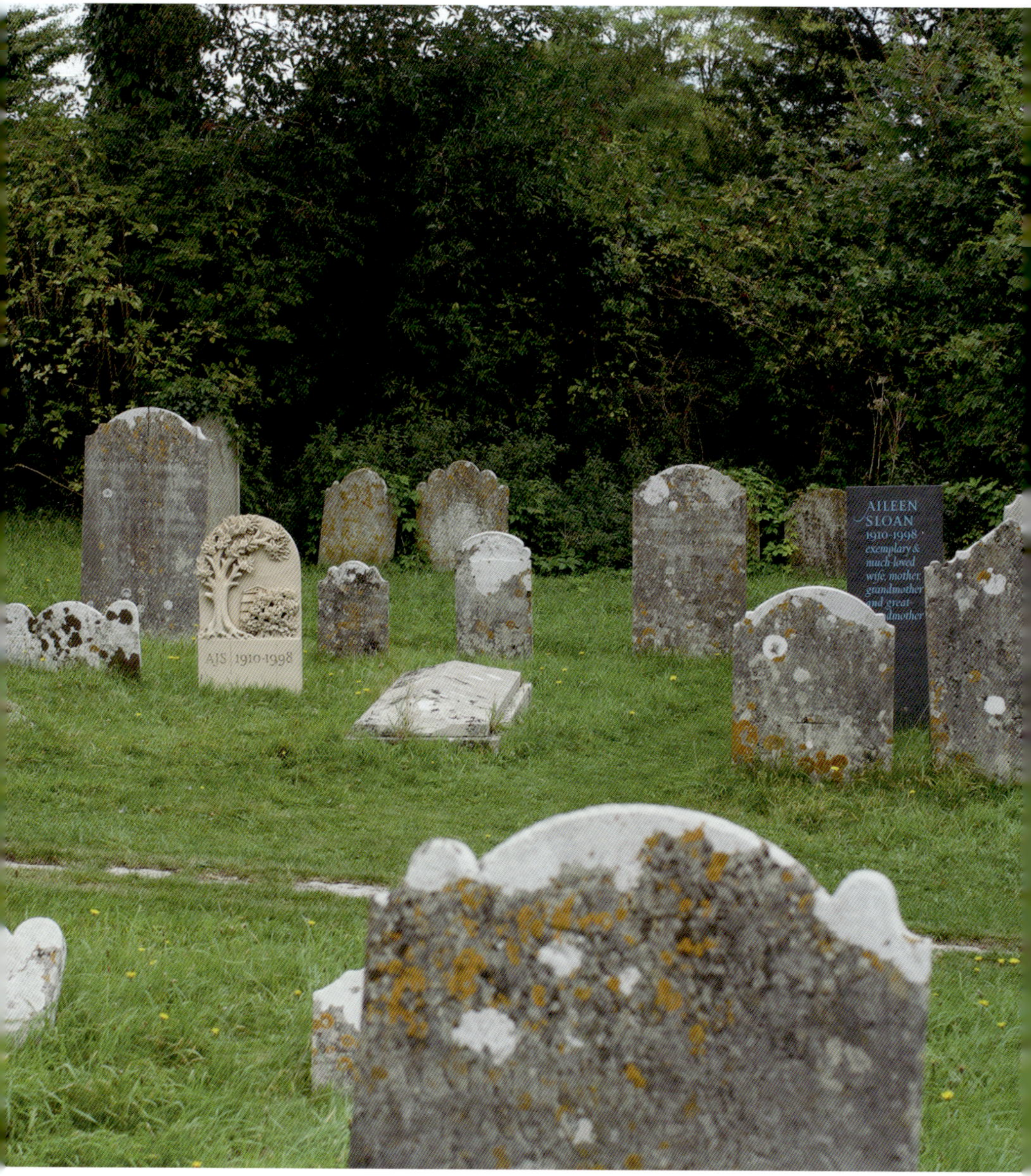
AJS | 1910-1998
AILEEN
SLOAN
1910-1998
exemplary &
much-loved
wife, mother,
grandmother
and great-

NICHOLAS SLOAN

Cast Iron 'Stone' to John Harrison
Cast Iron
915 x 455 x 20 mm

I wanted to use cast iron because I think it is a much undervalued material: adaptable, durable, can weather beautifully or be easily painted. It also appeals to me in being somehow honest and unassuming.

Secondly, I like the sturdy Egyptian or Clarendon letters that have traditionally been used for English cast-iron street names. I begin to find the restrained good taste of roman and italic on gravestones a little stifling. It is also a treat to revel in colour. There are contexts in which colourful memorials would look out of place, but I do think we have become too timid about exploiting the rich potential of colour.

Finally, it is good and fitting to be able to pay tribute to John Harrison, the stubborn genius whose infinite patience and ingenuity gave birth to the first reliable marine chronometer.

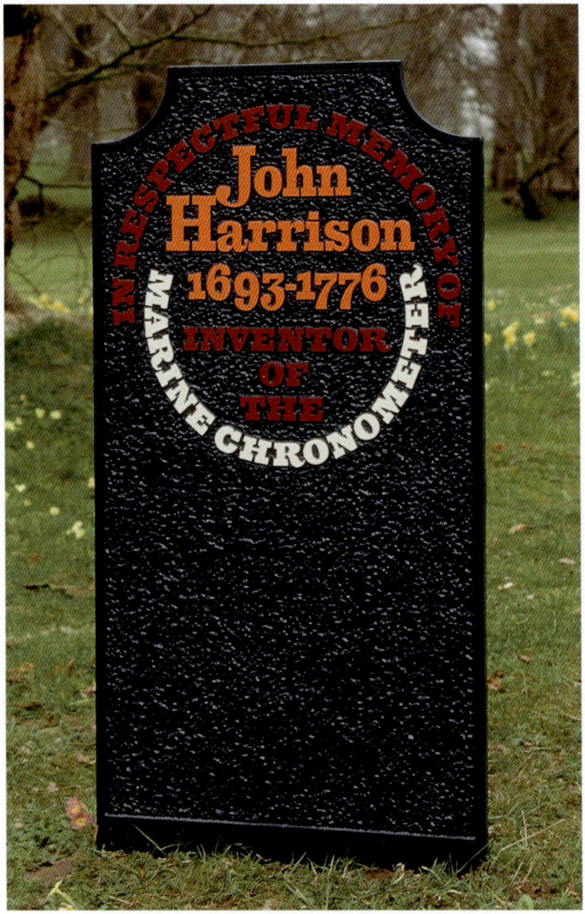

UNA SULLIVAN

Standing Stone
Riven Welsh Slate
1475 x 380 x 51

I like working on this kind of shape. It allows a lot of space to be left around the words, isolating them. I had no personal memorial to make, so it had to be something universal. I thought the word BLESS could stand on its own, outside of any particular context, but that it needed emphasising visually. I considered a gold line underneath to be appropriate, mirroring the feeling of the word BLESS as being a happy word. Although the gold line worked on paper and as a mental image, it had a surprisingly detrimental effect when actually used – detracting from the word so much that it virtually disappeared, and disassociating the space above from the space below. So the gold had to be cut away and the line left clean for the piece to work.

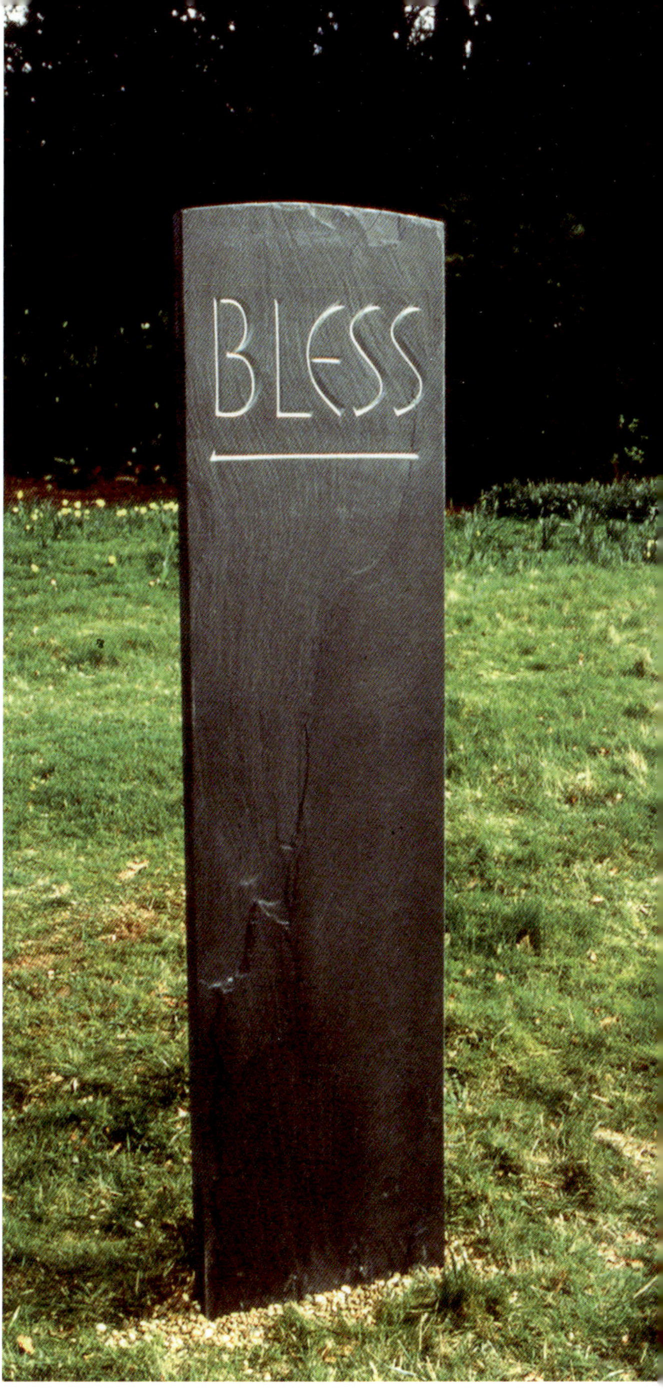

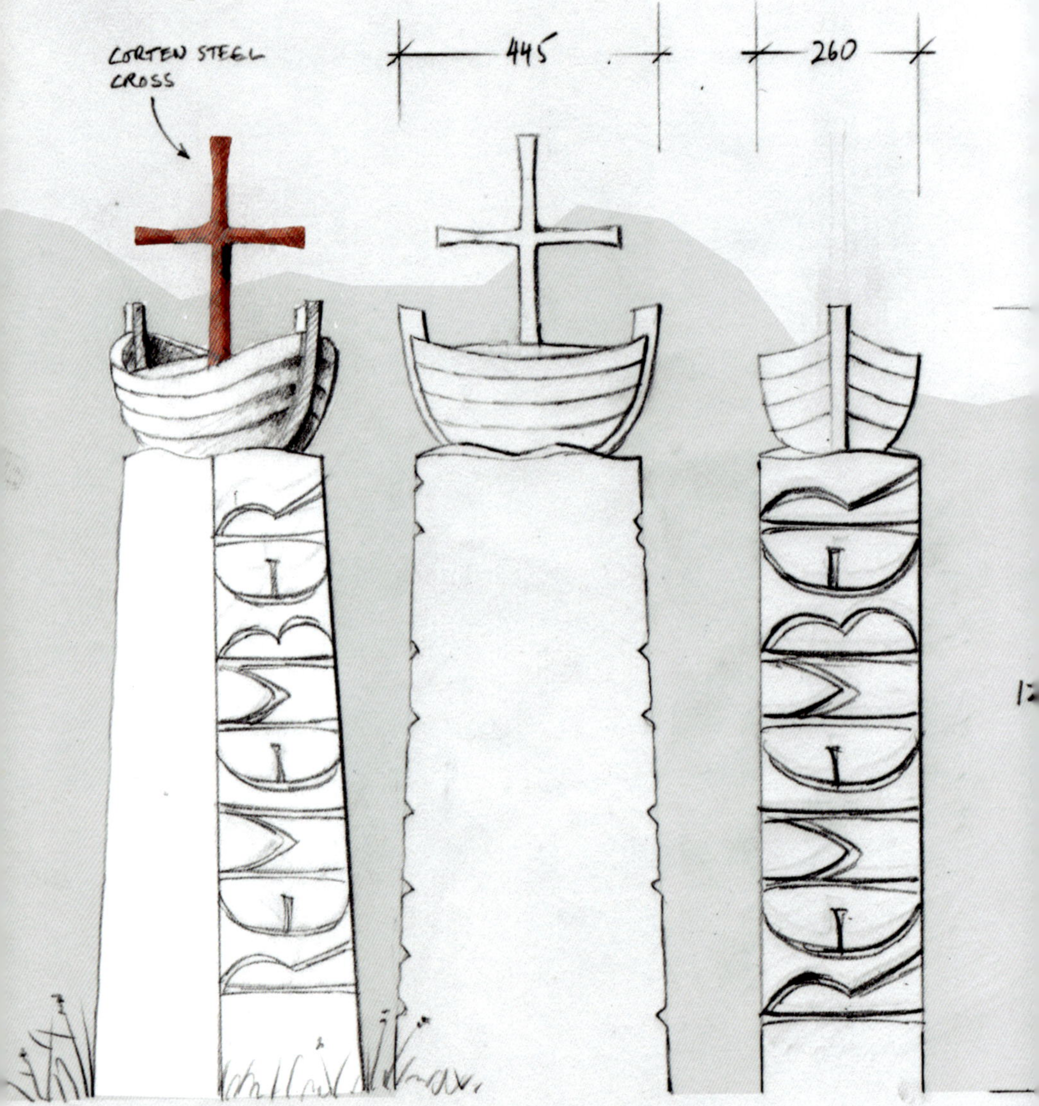

DESIGN PROPOSAL FOR GARDEN OF REMEMBRANCE MONUMENT
© GARY BREEZE FOR THE MEMORIAL ARTS CHARITY 22/2/10

GARY BREEZE

Garden of Remembrance Memorial
Crosland Hill Sandstone and Weathering (Cor-ten) Steel
1250 x 445 x 260mm

A garden of remembrance needs a point of focus, a memorial for everyone to identify with. This design was made in direct response to North Stoke church which is a very humble yet powerfully beautiful place. I wanted to design something quite small which would draw the bereaved or the visitor close to it. It needed to be something worthy of contemplation, an uplifting symbol of hope. I also wanted it to be unusual without being visually challenging; a recognisable image in an unusual context.

I have always been drawn to the Christian symbol of the boat, not simply as a safe haven from a stormy sea as an ark is, but as a means of journeying across it. The main part of a church building is called a nave after the Latin word for ship and it remains of course the emblem of the whole world Church. But for me the boat also represents *true* freedom, which always comes at a cost. Sailing is not the easy way, but ultimately, and if Nature/God permits, it can take you anywhere you want to go. The mast and yard arm form a simple cross made from weathering steel.

The best way to hone one's skill as a craftsperson is to make real commissions. The cost of the time and materials, combined with the expectations of the customer, will sharpen the wits more quickly than any amount of student practice. The Memorial Arts Charity is committed to helping the training of new craftspeople, and so as this memorial was to be commissioned by them, I felt it would be a good opportunity to give someone looking to improve their skills some on-the-job experience. Jo Sweeting is taking on the challenge under the skilled supervision of Christopher Elsey and Geoffrey Aldred at their workshop near Ditchling, West Sussex.

Garden of Remembrance monuments

The area set aside in a churchyard for the interment of ashes is usually called The Garden of Remembrance. It is becoming more and more common for this area to be marked with a central monument of some kind, rather than the usual small individual flat memorials, which take up more space and easily become very weathered and almost illegible (besides causing the usual problems when it comes to the mower). Some Garden of Remembrance monuments have the names of the deceased inscribed on them and others stand alone in memory of all whose ashes are placed there.

Gary Breeze's monument, illustrated opposite, is currently the most recent addition to The Art & Memory Collection.

The following four pages describe some other possibilities for Garden of Remembrance monuments.

GARDEN OF REMEMBRANCE MONUMENTS

Extracts from a letter (5 March 2010) from Ben Jones, lettercarver and sundial maker, to Harriet Frazer, after they had met to discuss ideas for Garden of Remembrance monuments:

'Cremation tablets need to be carefully set out or they can end up a bit of a jumble, and if the inscriptions on flat plaques are to be kept from being overgrown, they need lots of maintenance, especially grass-cutting. Many cemeteries and churchyards do not have the labour for this. One solution might be to get the lettering out of the damp ground and set it up vertically, gradually building a wall with the cremation stones as they arrive.

'The illustration below shows a nice stone wall. Each stone could have a name carved on it. Flowers could be planted at the foot of the wall and possibly in the wall, too. Many churchyard walls are listed and cannot be tampered with so it would have to be a new wall.

'Quite how a "wall of cremation stones" would be built would very much depend on the site itself, the local materials, who will manage the burials and how it will be financed. For instance it might be possible to build a complete new wall to start with. Then as each cremation took place a stone would be removed, inscribed and replaced. This sort of wall would cost a fair amount to begin with but with each new inscription the cost would be repaid over the years. If a churchyard needed a new wall this might be a useful solution. In another churchyard, for instance in Devon, where the "hedges" are earth banks, the new hedge would gradually be replaced by stones as the burials took place. Apart from the labour, the cost of building this hedge/wall would be relatively low and it would not matter how long it took to rebuild it in stone. Whichever way the wall is built, it needs to be carefully planned and for there to be someone who makes sure that the plan is kept to.

'Gates, gateposts, steps and styles are all good places for inscriptions and using them as memorials would help reduce the cost of a wall.

'The drawing below shows another wall where the inscriptions could be carved on the top face of the coping stones. Standard sized cremation tablets could be used. They could be sloped to shed rain water.

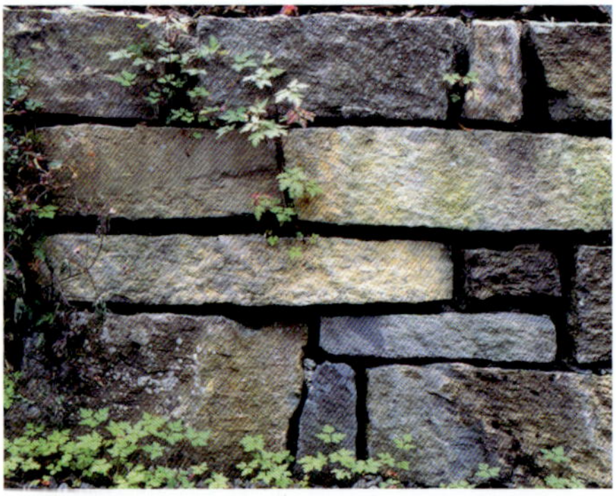

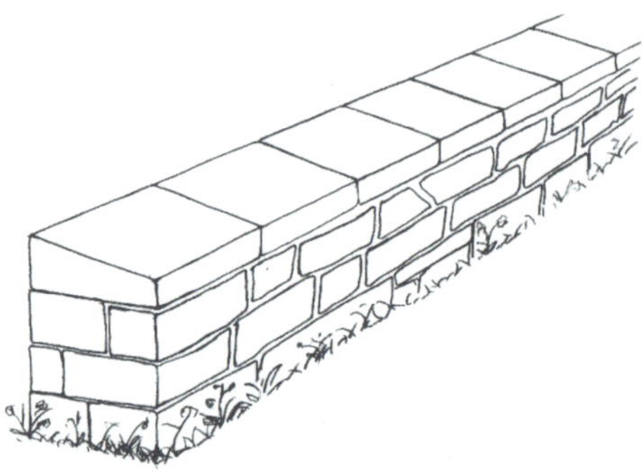

'The illustration below shows a pillar dial with faces on the north, south, east and west sides. The pillar itself would have names carved into it in spirals. Size and geometry might allow there to be one, two or more lines of names running down the column. If spiral grooves were carved down the column they would act as a guide to keep the letters in order. Inscriptions of odd lengths can be added to a spiral. Inscriptions could also be carved in the paving slabs surrounding the column. A lower cost option would be standard square plaque pavers, or plaques set in gravel on a foundation.

'My dial plinth made of diamonds would offer lots of faces for inscriptions if made large enough. It might be possible to make a column of rectangular blocks instead if the diamonds were thought too awkward a shape to carve inscriptions on.

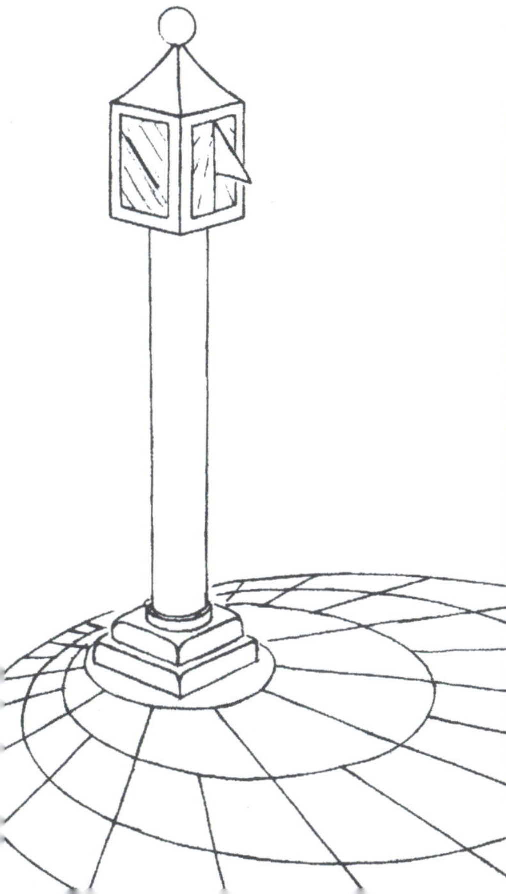

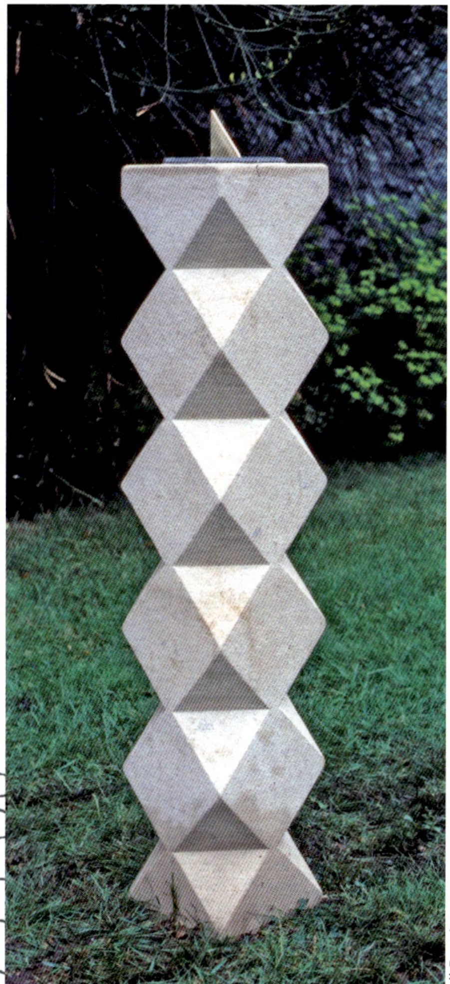

All Ben Jones

'The sundial below could be a much simpler affair with just a south facing dial, perhaps.'

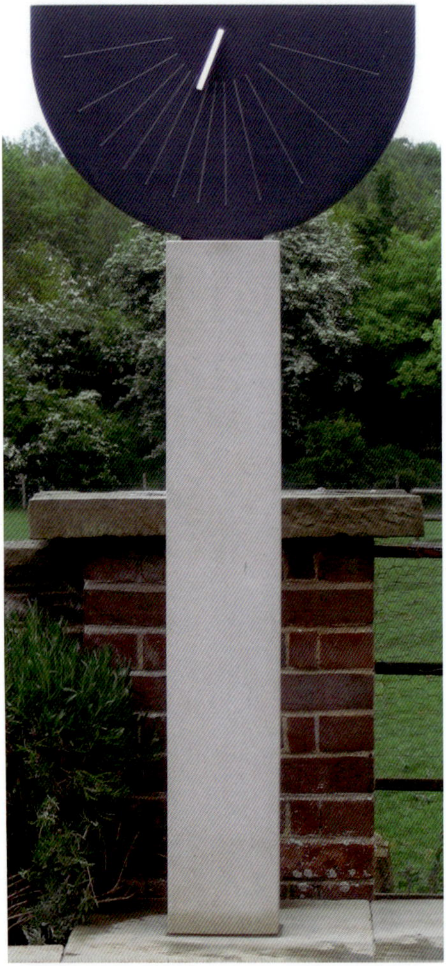

Ben Jones

The work opposite was commissioned by The Memorial Arts Charity for The Art of Remembering exhibition (Blickling Hall, Norfolk 1998). It was subsequently purchased by Father Roderick Hingley for the Memorial Garden in the churchyard of St Alban's, Romford, Essex.

Jamie Sargeant's statement for *The Art of Remembering* catalogue:

'A Garden of Remembrance memorial provides a place for names to be inscribed as the need arises. A point of rest in the churchyard reflecting dignity and continuity; regularly added to and yet remaining constant.

'This is one possible solution to the demands imposed on small parishes to meet a need within the constraints of a small budget. The column can carry at least 45–50 names – each being added below the last at the point where one ends and the next begins, thus creating an unpredictable texture.

'The design is based on simple geometric volumes – the cube, cylinder, sphere and cone – these being elemental forms symbolic of earth and spirit.'

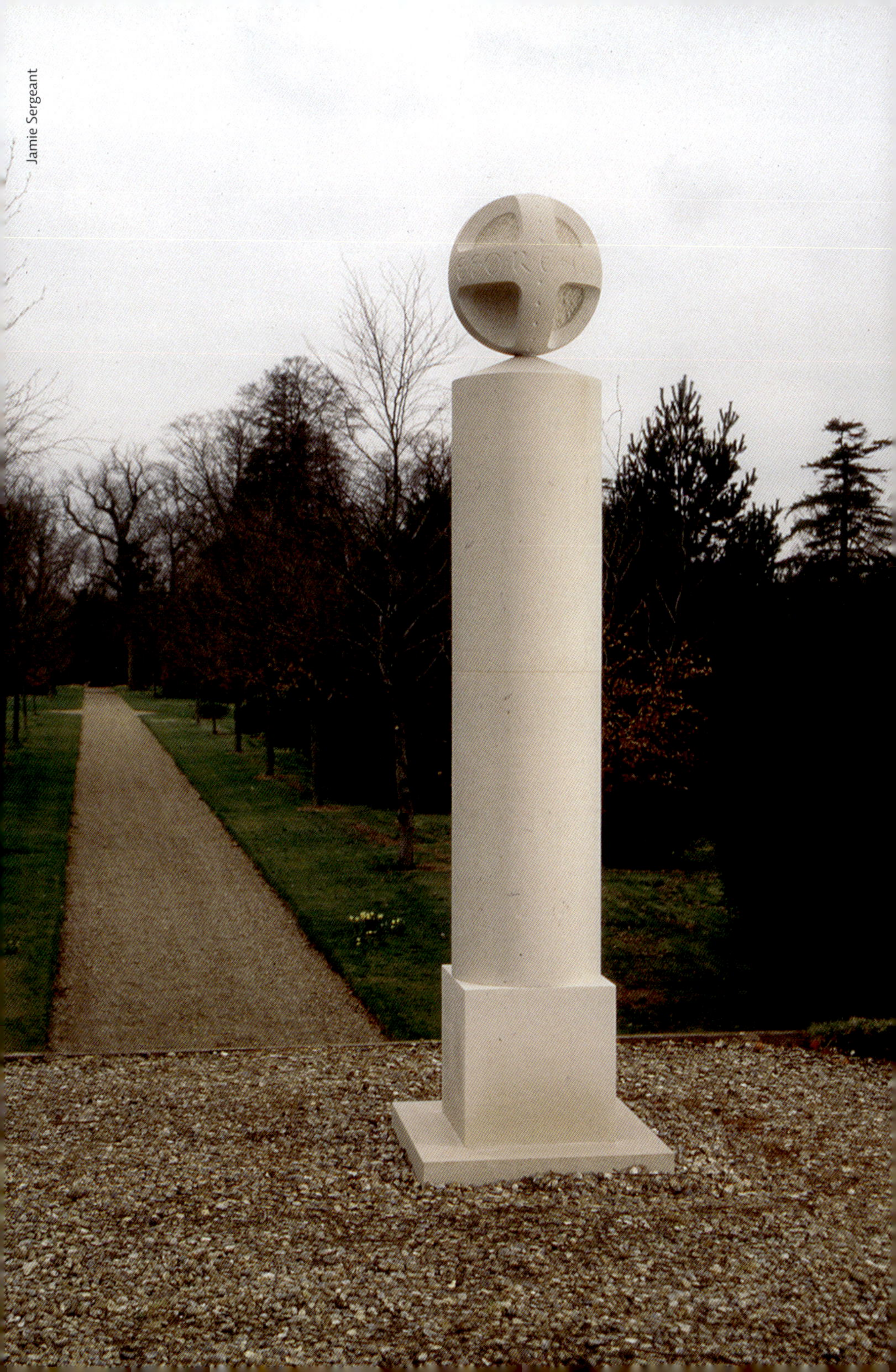

Jamie Sergeant

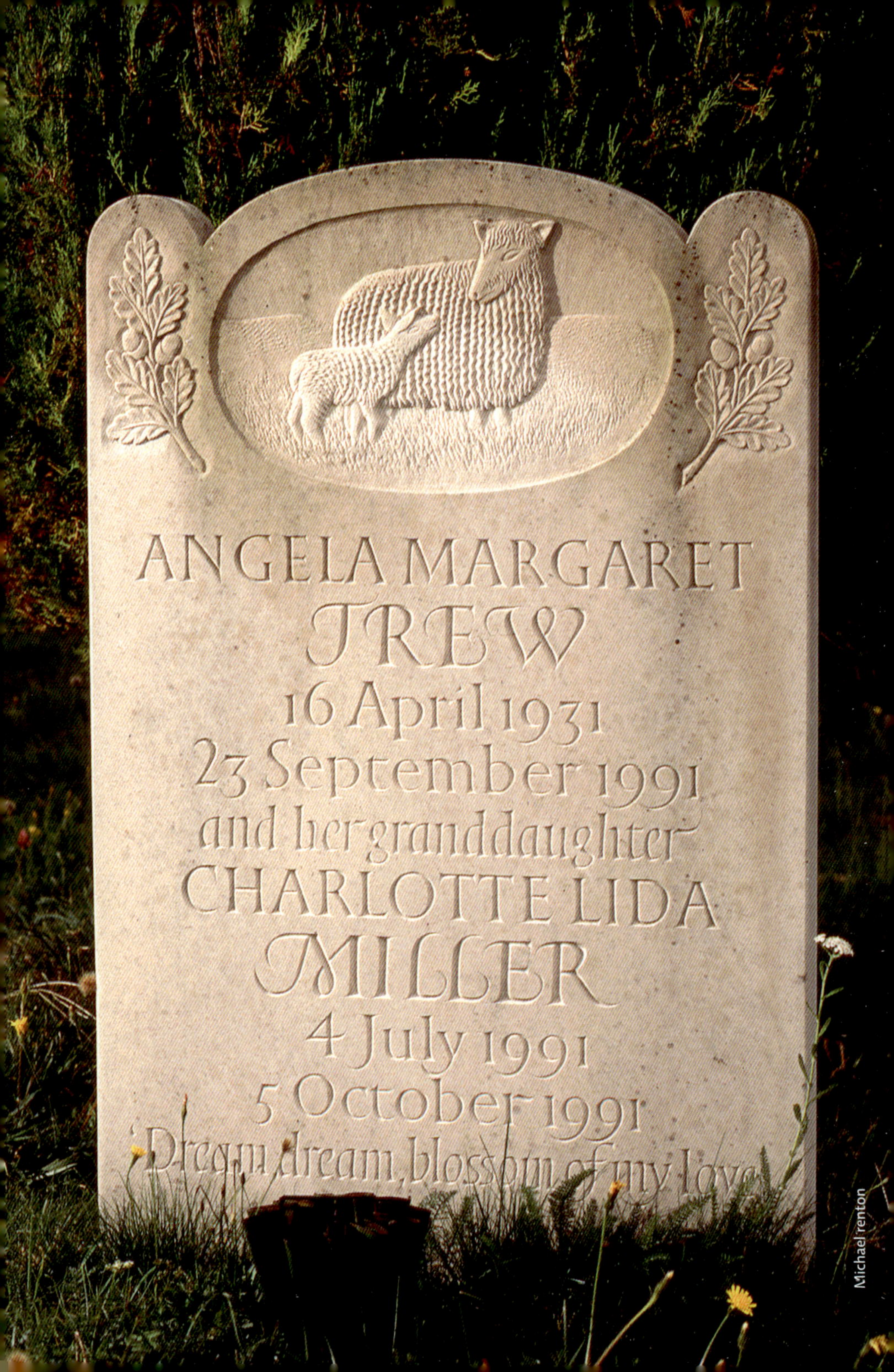

Michael renton

MEMORIALS BY ARTISTS

Helping people to commission unique memorials

Memorials by Artists was founded in 1988 to help people with the whole process of commissioning a well designed, unique memorial. We now have a register of around eighty lettercarvers who live and work throughout the British Isles and also in Ireland.

Memorials by Artists has evolved through various forms since it was first established but a constant feature has been the series of fully illustrated publications, including our book for young people's memorials*. These books include several articles on the subject giving information and advice about materials, weathering, wording, different styles of memorials and so on; also showing much of the best work being done in this field. The aim has always been to enlighten and inform anyone interested in having a good, individual memorial made.

In the earlier days we only offered one service, which we now call the Fully Guided service. This involves overseeing the project from start to finish but, importantly, without interfering in the collaboration between artist and client which is so vital to the success of the whole process. However with the advent of the internet it became clear that we needed to offer more choice and we now offer an Introductory service as well as the new Find Your Own Way service. The latter, a free service via the internet, enables people to look at a great variety of work and to make their own choice of lettercarver.

* See page 64 for a list of our publications.

NAMES, DATES & EPITAPHS Simon Frazer

Carved lettering has its own quality, somewhere between the graphic and the sculptural, and can give the words we choose unexpected levels of weight and meaning.

But what words do we choose? Traditionally a memorial inscription may be made up of several distinct parts, which are differentiated from each other in size and style of lettering, and in the overall design.

First, often omitted these days, is a formulaic introduction such as 'In Loving Memory', or the 'Sacred to the Memory' that we see on 19th century memorials, often carved in an extravagant calligraphic or decorative style.

The next element is the name, the most important and, with the dates, regarded as the only essential wording on the stone. It fulfils the function of the memorial as record and marker. But more than that it asserts, and in a sense stands for the existence of the person who has gone. This is why the form of name is so significant: for many it seems natural to use the name by which a person was actually known, such as a nickname or an abbreviation. The central significance of the name is usually acknowledged by its lettering and position on the memorial.

Sometimes names and dates are the only inscribed features on a stone; this need not lessen its interest. The memorials in this exhibition provide a fascinating range of lettering styles. There are some fine versions of traditional letterforms, with other more idiosyncratic alphabets; each one has its own formal and expressive qualities.

A decision to be made regarding the dates is whether to include the days and months with the years. The years alone can make for a stronger design, but in some instances the date may have special significance and be worth recording.

After the name and dates the next part of the inscription is generally referred to as the epitaph, which traditionally might have had several sections, each with a different emphasis. Broadly speaking the purposes of an epitaph are to praise, mourn and console. Nowadays few epitaphs take the form of a formal eulogy but praise is implicit in the short descriptive tags which often follow the name – solid words celebrating value in activities and relationships: 'writer', 'churchwarden', 'beekeeper', 'husband and father'. Sometimes the praise is more explicitly expressed in a simple, strong statement, whether reflecting public achievement 'A rare singer' or a private vision 'Flower of Light'.

Mourning and consolation too are likely to be expressed obliquely on modern memorials, by means of a quotation or a carved symbol. In an age when we are confronted constantly by written messages, signs and slogans, the understated and the genuine gain an added power, just as the grave site itself is understood to be a place set apart, where the visitor is likely to be receptive to stillness and contemplation.

On some memorials, especially to those who died tragically young, the

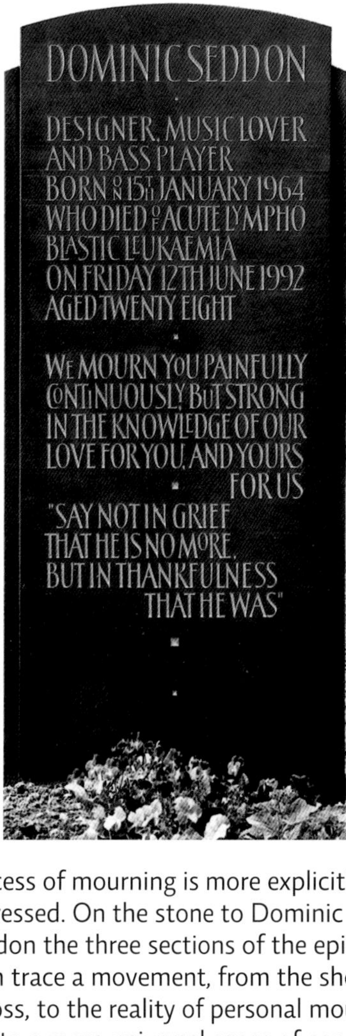

Gary Breeze

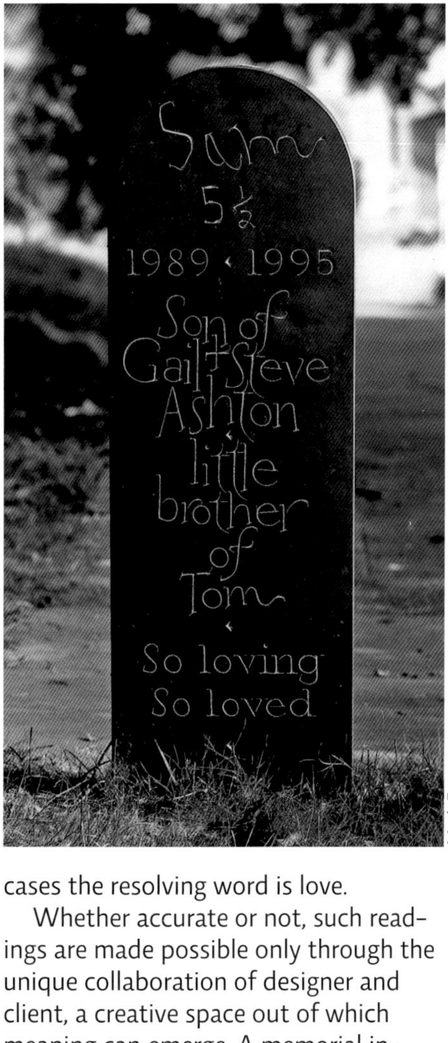

Mark Evans

process of mourning is more explicitly expressed. On the stone to Dominic Seddon the three sections of the epitaph trace a movement, from the shock of loss, to the reality of personal mourning, to a more universal sense of consolation. We could read a similar movement in the stone to Sam Ashton, headed by Sam's own signature carved on to the slate, which is both vivid and personal and visually jagged and asymmetrical. The lettering of the inscription suggests a process of re-establishing a sense of balance and with it a degree of acceptance and continuity. In both these cases the resolving word is love.

Whether accurate or not, such readings are made possible only through the unique collaboration of designer and client, a creative space out of which meaning can emerge. A memorial inscription by its nature is a public statement, but just as the stone marks a private territory, the words on it bear witness to a private ceremony, in which a life is celebrated and symbolically completed. It is a message on a frontier.

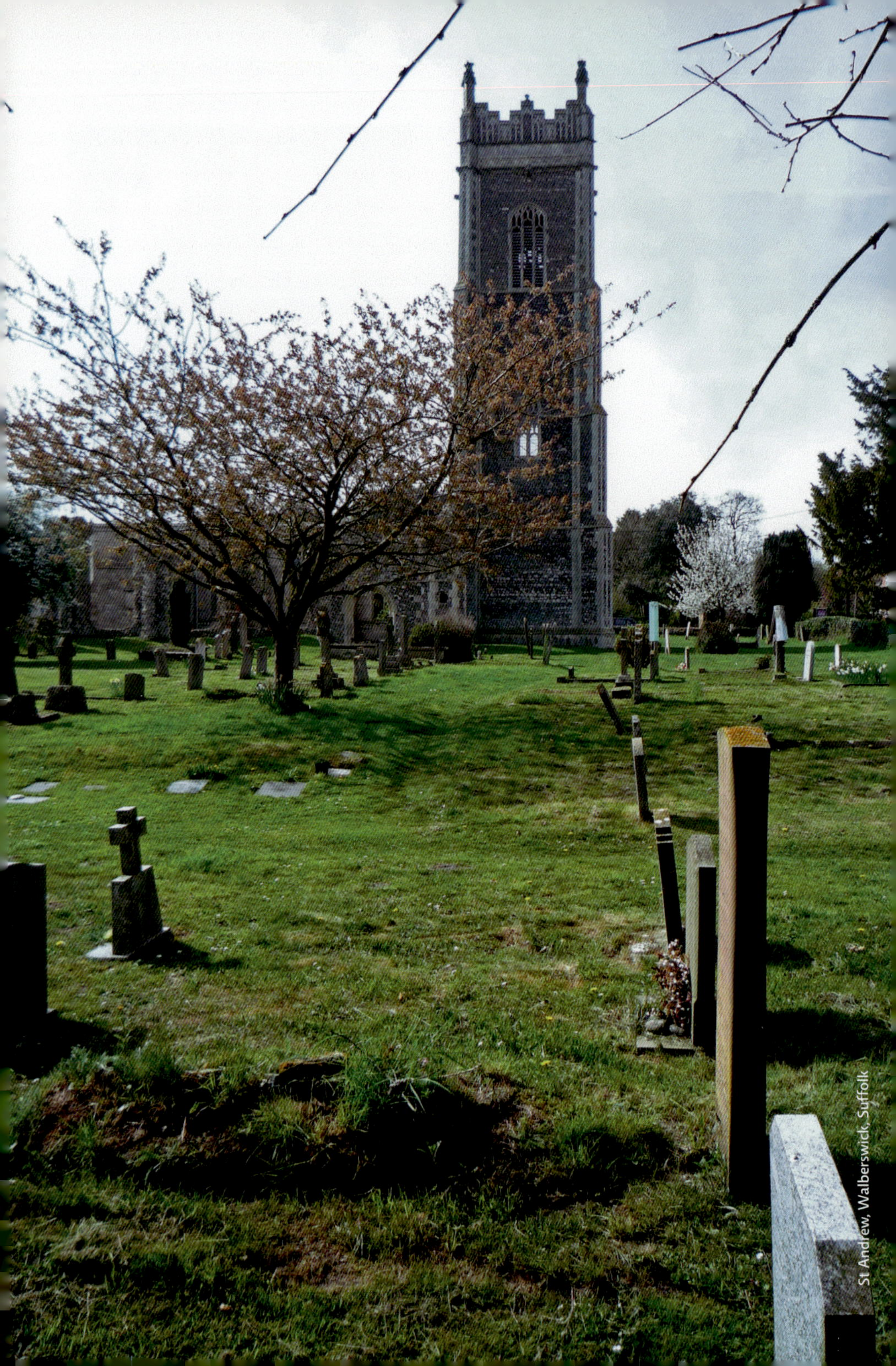
St Andrew, Walberswick, Suffolk

APPLYING FOR PERMISSION FOR A CHURCHYARD MEMORIAL

Unless you have had previous experience of commissioning a memorial it can come as some surprise to find out that churchyards and cemeteries across the country are governed by rules and regulations. These may encompass such things as the material used (*eg* limestone, sandstone, granite, slate or wood), the height, width and thickness of the stone, the method of installation and, most importantly for memorials which are to be erected in churchyards, the content of the inscription or carving.

An application to erect a churchyard memorial must be made to the vicar of the parish on a specific form of application. It is important to make sure that permission has been granted before ordering the stone from the quarry. If the design of the memorial comes within the diocesan rules and regulations, the vicar is normally able to grant permission without further ado.

A diocese is a district under the pastoral care of a bishop. There are 43 dioceses in England, which cover all 48 counties. For churchyard memorials each diocese has its own set of rules which are drawn up by an independent judge known as the Chancellor. Some diocesan rules are fairly lenient; others much more restrictive.

If the vicar feels that the memorial application falls outside the diocesan regulations he will let you know and discuss the way forward with you. You may wish to change the design in order to obtain approval. Alternatively, you may wish to apply for a faculty, which is the ecclesiastical equivalent to planning permission. Again your vicar will guide you on how to go about this.

Cemeteries are usually run by district, town or local councils who publish the rules for individual burial grounds. There is normally much more freedom, at least as far as wording and carving are concerned, than in a churchyard. However, there will almost always be restrictions on size.

Some people have told us that if they had known about the rules and regulations for memorials before making a decision about the burial they would have chosen differently. So if a decision has yet to be made, about whether to choose your local churchyard or cemetery, it would be worthwhile researching the different options, and giving some thought to the type of memorial you might wish to have and whether your ideas for it would be allowed.

ADVICE FROM THE CHURCHYARDS HANDBOOK

The most striking feature of any churchyard is likely to be the monuments, whether these are elaborate chest tombs or simple headstones. Monuments are a solace to the relatives of the people they commemorate; visitors come to look at them and passers by pause to read. They embody the social history of a community and form a tangible expression of its roots. Most importantly, they express the purpose of the churchyard as a place where the mortal remains of past generations of Christian people are reverently laid and their earthly lives recorded.

The law regulating what monuments may be erected, and also what may happen to them later, has important implications for Christian ministry. Regrettably, monuments can sometimes cause dissension or misunderstanding, particularly where relatives are not allowed to erect the type of stone or to have carved the inscription that they have chosen. The designs proposed may not only lack aesthetic distinction but take little account of the essential Christian nature of a churchyard. On the other hand, it may be pastorally difficult to refuse an unsatisfactory memorial if that is likely to cause resentment and distress.

Monuments are also of concern for historical and artistic reasons and because of the pleasure that they give to the public. Conservation societies and individual enthusiasts expect protection for the settings of ancient churches and a high quality for any additions. This may conflict with the pastoral need to accord with the individual wishes of the bereaved, especially where a person being commemorated had a real connection with the church.

It can be argued that the repetitive nature of modern churchyard memorials is a result of too much restriction in what is allowed. This argument can be challenged by reference to the many well-designed memorials that fall within the terms of what is normally allowed. However, while churchyard regulations can exclude what is seen as undesirable or unreasonable, they cannot of themselves ensure the creation of good designs.

Independent lettercutters have reported difficulty in getting their designs accepted by parish clergy for three main reasons:

Some clergy are wary of designs that are at all out of the ordinary, and advise the person commissioning the memorial that a faculty will be required, when in fact the memorial does fall within the standard provisions that the clergy are allowed to authorize locally. For example, simple embellishment depicting religious or occupational symbolism may be deemed to need a faculty, since the relevant churchyard rules require faculties for statuary, whereas the rule is intended to apply only to three-dimensional carving.

Regrettably some clergy seem to resent spending time dealing with memorial applications, regarding it as a distraction from their 'real' work. The more out of the ordinary the application, the more likely they are to display this attitude. Perhaps more could be done to encourage the view that a memorial is an important part of the grieving process, and is a pastoral opportunity, even if the people concerned are not members of the local congregation.

It must be admitted that efforts to avoid the restless and discordant effect of inappropriately shaped and sized stones can result in uniform rows of very similar headstones, lacking the character of earlier memorials. There is much to be said for encouraging variety, as long as the emphasis remains on quality.

There are specific restrictions within some diocesan churchyard rules stipulating minimum sizes. These were introduced following advice in earlier years, not least in earlier editions of *The Churchyards Handbook*, to curb what were seen as the excesses of many memorials of the late nineteenth and early twentieth centuries. Nowadays this advice may no longer be appropriate as it may rule out – other than by faculty – a well designed slender memorial.

It will produce better results in the long term if those responsible for churchyards are encouraged to welcome creative and individual designs and to focus the churchyard regulations on excluding that which would be genuinely out of keeping, for instance by inappropriate materials or size. Precise dimensions can be left to the good sense of the designer, always bearing in mind that the parish priest can refer for faculty decision anything about which he or she is genuinely unhappy. In doubtful cases the parish priest would be advised to seek advice from the Archdeacon or Diocesan Advisory Committee secretary, who may well be able to give an encouraging or warning word.

Inscriptions

The theological implications of an inscription are important but the issues of social usage can prove even more controversial. The use of familiar or colloquial terms on memorials raises strong feelings. For many, the description of someone as 'A devoted and much loved dad and granddad' is the natural expression of the feelings he evoked in life; for others such language is over familiar for what is a public statement.

It must be acknowledged that in all areas of life, informal modes are becoming preferred to formal. Maintaining the standard of earlier years can be misinterpreted as snobbery or insensitivity. It is vital that any restrictions are imposed consistently. A practice may be forbidden in one particular churchyard, even if it is permitted elsewhere in the diocese, but any exception will seem unfair to those who have previously been denied it.

Inevitably churchyard regulations will sometimes be seen as negative and obstructive. However, when they work properly, they enable both the bereaved and the Church to conduct their affairs more easily.

Edited extracts from Chapters 4 & 8 of *The Churchyards Handbook*, Thomas Cocke FSA (ed.) Church House Publishing 2001

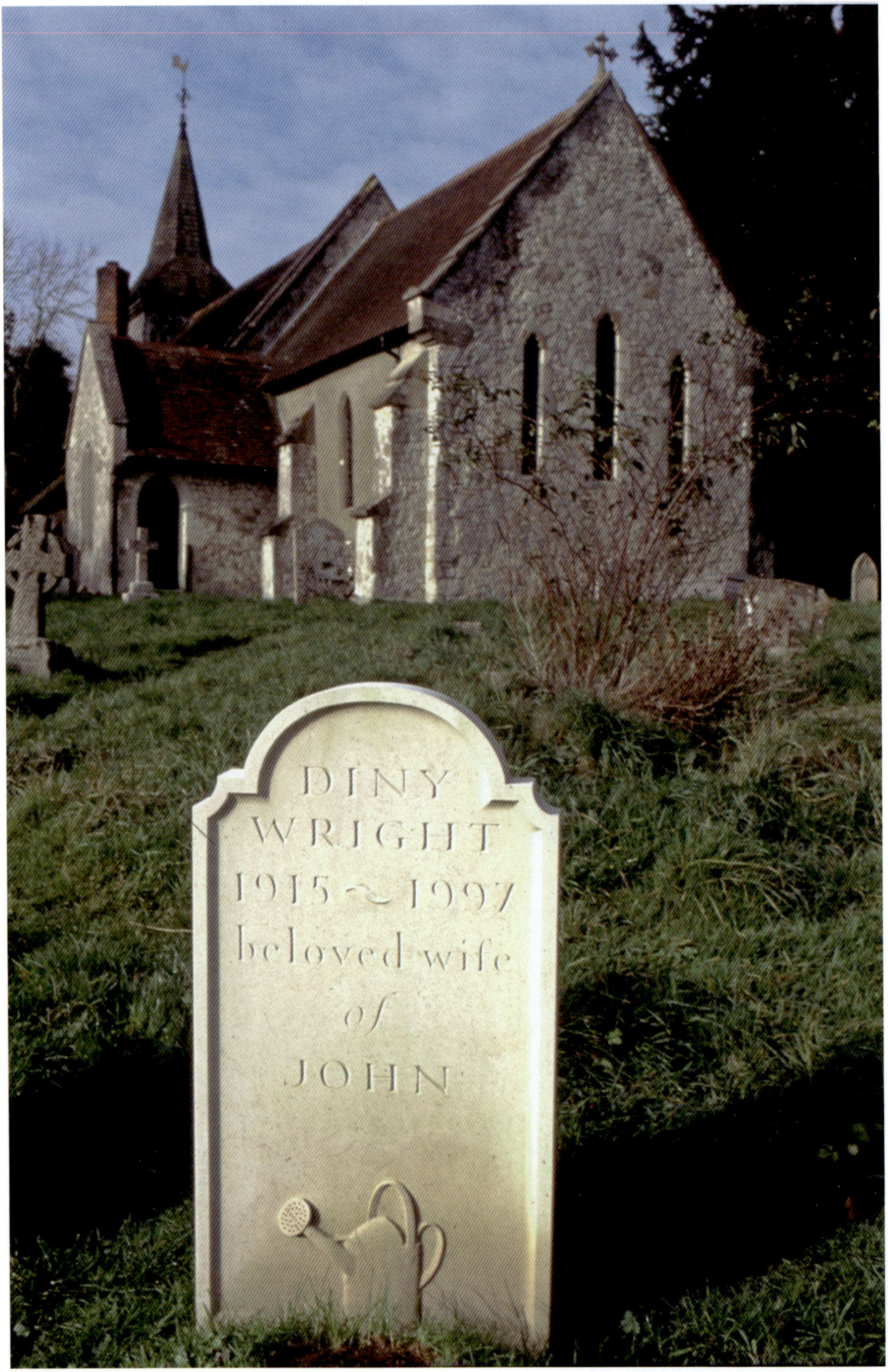

Andrew Whittle

THE GENTLE ART OF REGULATION

The Worshipful Christopher Clark QC

It is twelve years since I first put pen to paper on this subject. How far the theme of my original article has been put into general practice is difficult to say. Most of the Chancellors I know take a similar, relatively informal, but sensible attitude to Churchyard Regulations. But there are places, I fear, where applying to introduce an artistic memorial outside the norm becomes a tedious and frustrating bureaucratic headache.

To put into practice this quote, 'The Gentle Art of Regulation', in both dioceses of which I am Chancellor, I try to avoid the dead hand of bureaucracy. Incumbents are allowed a degree of latitude in permitting memorials in churchyards for which they are responsible. Where, however, a proposed memorial falls well outside my guidelines, I invite details of the proposal to be sent straight to me. I am then in a position to indicate informally whether it is acceptable.

It is only when a proposal is controversial (*eg* when the Parochial Church Council object to it, yet the proposer still wishes to go ahead), that I insist upon the formal faculty process being used. In approaching matters in this way, I endeavour to keep paperwork to a minimum. Grieving families have enough on their minds. There is no need to add to their heavy burden.

Grief can be such an intense emotion. Sooner or later we all have personal experience of it. As mourners, we may feel strongly about the design of a particular gravestone and the wording on it. Moreover, we live in an age when people expect to be allowed to commemorate their nearest and dearest as they see fit: 'If a young man who was keen on motor cycles was killed in a road accident, why should he not have a motor cycle carved on his headstone?'.

To many, what is appropriate in a churchyard is a matter of taste. Your taste is different from my taste. Why should a diocesan Chancellor or an Advisory Committee be permitted to dictate matters of taste to an emotionally upset and vulnerable group of people like a grieving family?

These are questions which should be faced by any Chancellor or other person responsible for enforcing churchyard rules and regulations. Speaking for myself, I do not, in fact, regard it as part of my professional function to dictate matters of taste. It is, however, part of my function to supervise what is permitted within churchyards. So how do I approach the task?

I work on the principal that I want to encourage harmony: harmony between one gavestone and another; harmony between gravestones and the churchyard as a whole; harmony between the churchyard and the church. Harmony does not equate with uniformity. Churchyards are not war cemeteries. The last thing I am seeking is exactly the same size of stone, or shape, or colour, or design, or lettering. There is much room for individuality. In particular, I welcome and encourage memorials of artistic design with good lettering.

Nevertheless, in seeking harmony, I have to apply a test. I call it the 'sore thumb' test. If a proposal stands out like a sore thumb, it should not be allowed.

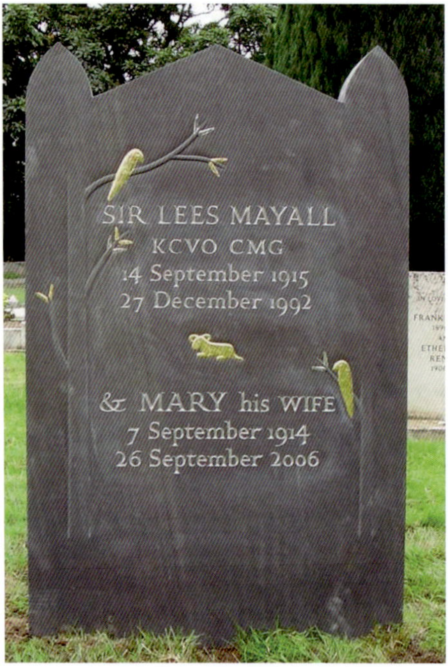

Designed by Craigie Aitchison and carved by The Verity Workshop

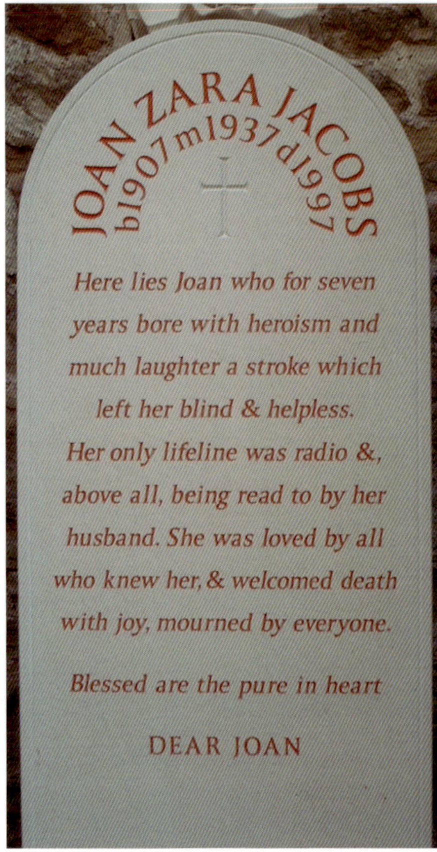

Designed by Andrew Grassby, machine-engraved with Michael Harvey's Grassby Roman font

Let me give an example: polished stone is becoming more and more popular. A series of polished black granite or white marble headstones in a local authority cemetery may be acceptable. But put a polished marble or granite headstone alongside the wall of a mediaeval church and it would stand out dreadfully. There would be no harmony between the headstone and the church.

As for designs or motifs like, say, the motorcycle referred to earlier, one has to be particularly careful and sensitive. Some think such designs or motifs out of place in a Christian churchyard. On the other hand, if the bereaved are desperately keen and the designer can incorporate the request simply and unobtrusively, there may well be an argument for saying it should be permitted. This is where sensitive and tactful discussion between the bereaved, the incumbent and the churchwardens may lead to an agreed solution which, if necessary, can be put before the Chancellor for approval.

Likewise with inscriptions, I strongly believe that an incumbent must listen to the views of mourners and discuss sympathetically with them what would be the appropriate wording on a memorial. Many would say that inscriptions should reflect the fashion of the age. Victorian and surviving earlier

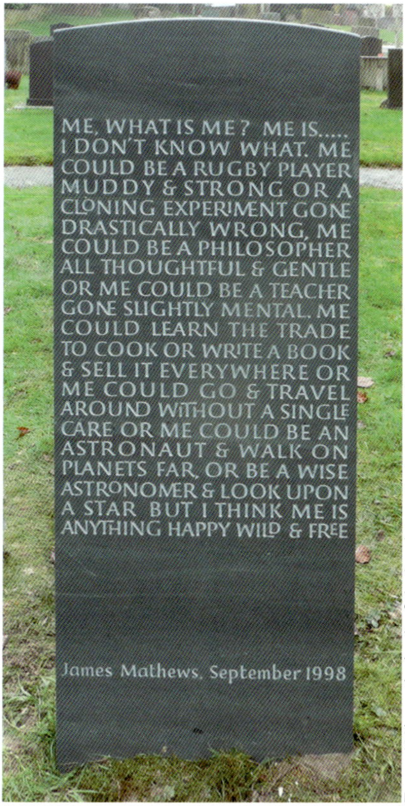

Teucer Wilson: the back of the headstone to James Mathews, aged 12

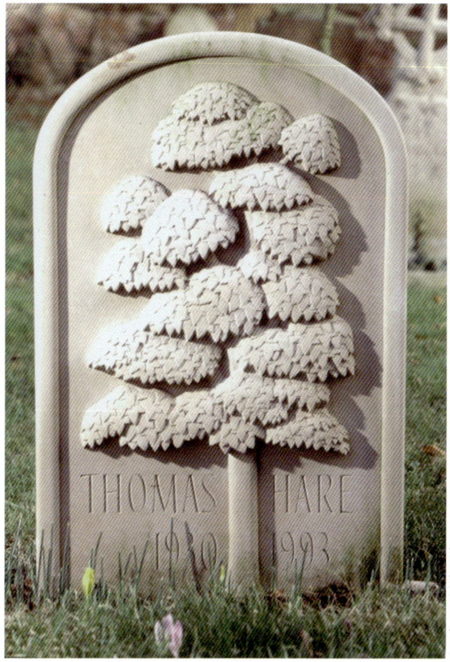

Andrew Whittle

inscriptions reflect periods when the English language was generally used in a grander, more expansive way. A tendency towards less formal inscriptions is the fashion at the present time. If the family want it, is 'Bill' as opposed to 'William' really objectionable? I myself draw the line at nicknames on their own, simply because, if members of a family wish a person to be buried in a Christian churchyard, they should expect his/her memorial to have his/her Christian name on it. If a Christian name, however, is followed by a nickname, is that truly objectionable? For family and friends, the nickname may be an important part of the memorial, and for onlookers it adds to the interest without, in my view, standing out offensively.

Many of our churchyards are truly beautiful places. They are not however, to be preserved in aspic. New graves will be needed; new memorials will be commissioned. In response, carvers and masons can use their imagination and skill to create fine and enduring works of art. The truly exceptional memorials in this exhibition show the quality of what can be achieved. Depending upon the particular churchyard and its environment, such memorials ought, in principle, to be permitted without delay or argument.

Revised and edited version of 'The gentle art of regulation', *The Art of Remembering* (ex.cat.) Carcanet 1998

Christopher Clark QC, is Chancellor of the Dioceses of Winchester and Portsmouth.

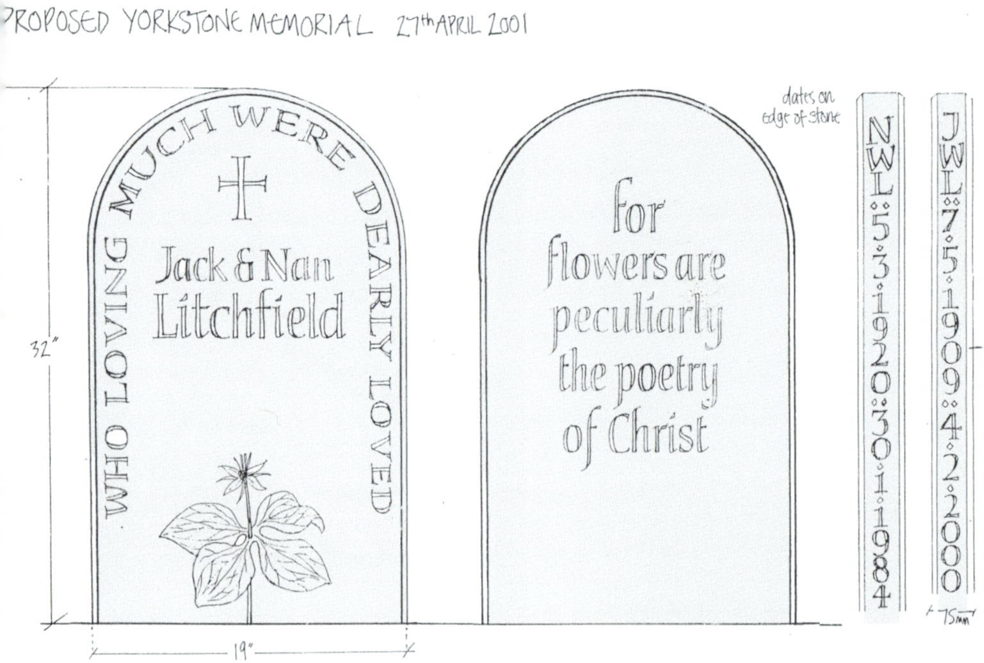

Teucer Wilson

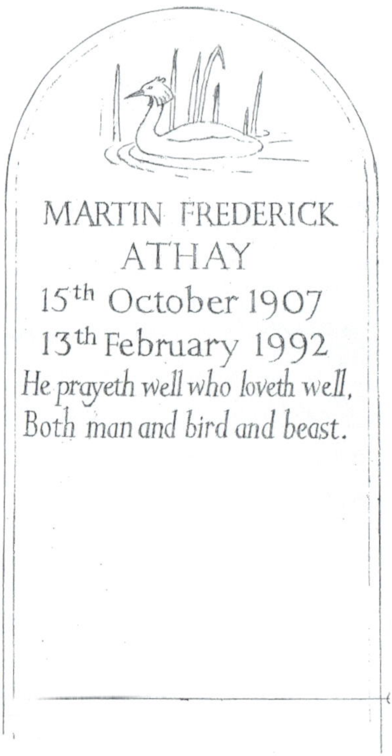

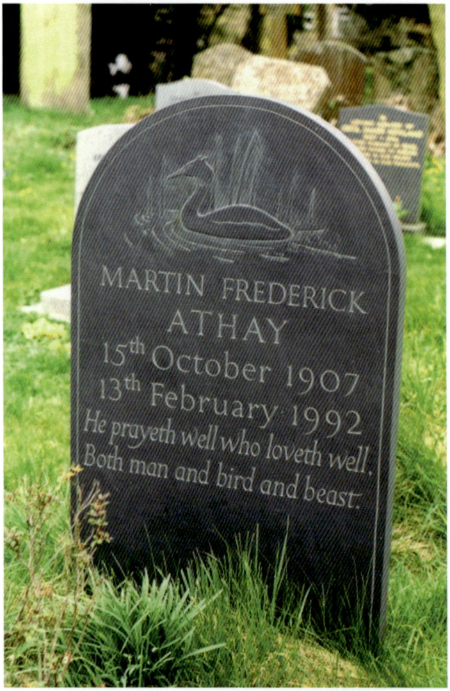

Peter Foster

'UNUSUAL' MEMORIALS AND THE CHURCHYARD RULES

Harriet Frazer

We are well aware of the difficulties the clergy can have over granting permission for churchyard memorials – for instance, when a family wants to introduce a polished granite memorial with gold lettering into the churchyard; or equally, when the design for a memorial is at all 'unusual' – a word that often crops up in connection with proposals from independent lettercarvers. From our experience, it seems that many members of the clergy do not feel sufficiently sure of their ground on this subject and are fearful of introducing anything other than standard run-of-the-mill memorials into their churchyards. On the other hand, one incumbent, who looks after several parishes, told me that he would, 'rather have the Archdeacon rap my knuckles than cause pastoral problems'. The whole situation is tricky indeed and can cause a great deal of unhappiness for the bereaved and pastoral difficulties for clergy. When a faculty (ecclesiastical planning permission) does have to be applied for, there are additional costs to pay and often a four to nine month wait to hear the verdict. People can easily give up at this stage, settle for less than they had wanted, and turn away from the Church. The fourth edition *Churchyards Handbook* gives much helpful advice on how to deal with these sensitive issues. (See also pages 46–51).

The illustrations in this article show a few examples of cases where the permission procedure has not been straightforward.

Headstone to Jack & Nan Litchfield

The incumbent said he found the design 'quite pleasing' but that he could only grant permission for 'simple' memorials, so a faculty would have to be applied for. A long correspondence ensued. Four months later the faculty was granted and we heard that the Chancellor was 'very fond of the poem by Christopher Smart and very pleased to grant the faculty'.

Headstone to Martin Athay

In this case the rector had thought the grebe was 'a little too large' so he had written to the Diocesan Registrar for advice. The Registrar wrote back to say he was inclined to agree about the size of the grebe but that he was more concerned about whether the grebe was an 'image' or a 'symbol' – symbols being allowed in the churchyard rules but not images. The registrar replied: 'Is the Grebe an 'image'? I would say not, but I am not sure why. I am not anxious to delay matters, but I think that I should refer the design to the Diocesan Advisory Committee and then, perhaps, to the Chancellor.'

Three months later we heard from the incumbent that the Diocesan Advisory Committee had 'warmly recommended' the design and that there would be no need to apply for a faculty.

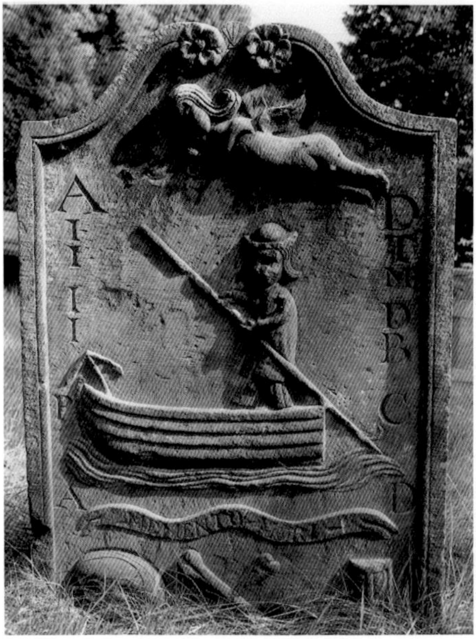

Kinnoull, Perthshire, 1772

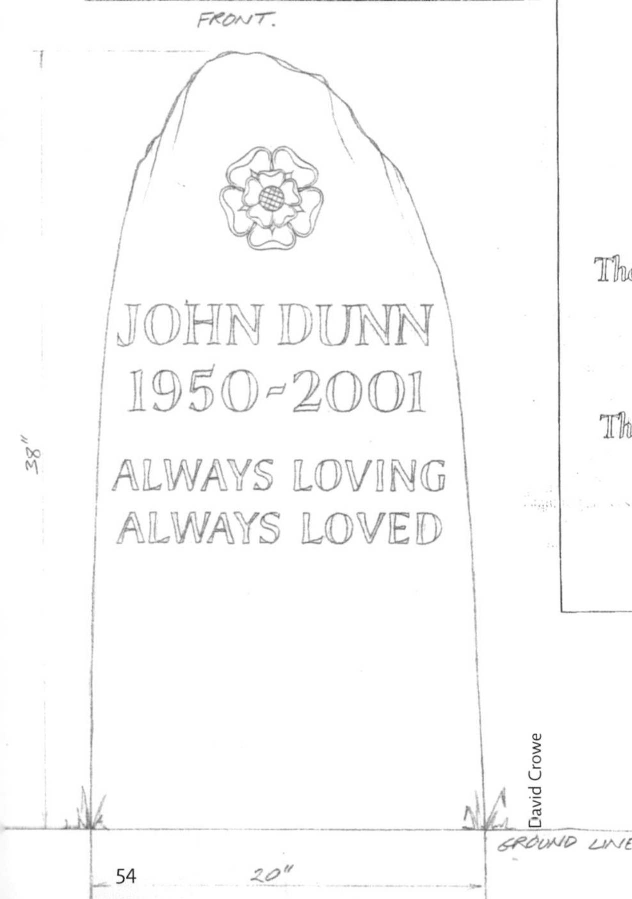

David Crowe

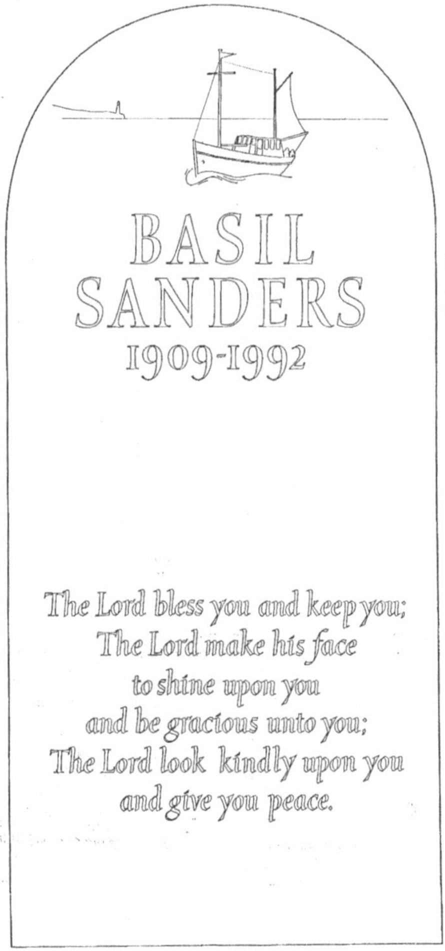

Nicholas Sloan

Headstone to Basil Sanders

The Diocesan Registrar decided that the design did not conform to the regulations, which only allowed 'simple decoration', and that a faculty would have to be applied for. A long correspondence ensued between the family of the deceased, the vicar, the Registrar, the Diocesan Secretary and the designer of the headstone. The family felt strongly that 'something simple and private has been made unnecessarily complicated and public'; the vicar that he was not qualified to make 'legal or aesthetic judgements'; the Registrar that he was 'not certain that the design could be considered to fall within the description "simple decoration"', and the designer of the memorial that, 'to allow a common sense view to prevail would avoid a lot of distress. It really does seem unjust that a small carving of a fishing boat should be considered to necessitate the drawing up of an expensive legal document to permit Mrs Sanders to place a stone outside the church that she and her late husband have each served for forty years'.

Edited extract from a later letter from the maker of the memorial to the Registrar:

'I have been making gravestones for about twenty years. I became involved in this partly because I think that many of the early gravestones in English churchyards are among the most beautiful artefacts around, and I like working in that tradition. Like most serious lettercutters, I am very conscious of the sites of the stones that I make. I am anxious that they should complement the churchyards in which they find themselves. Therefore, I am conscious of churchyards in general, and I deplore most of what I see currently being introduced to them. Clearly the Church shares this concern, and yet too often I hear of difficulties between representatives of the Church and lettercutters who are genuinely trying to raise the standards of memorials: perhaps the two classes of people who most have the good interests of churchyards at heart. Please may I ask you very seriously to consider whether your procedures do not sometimes stand in the way of your objectives in encouraging good design?'

That a faculty would be granted was apparently never in question but the procedure still had to be gone through and took over nine months from start to finish. The cost today (2010) would be £215.

Headstone to John Dunn

Mrs Dunn was very clear from the outset of the commission that she wanted a 'traditional but slightly asymmetrical memorial with a carving of a Yorkshire rose' in Cumbrian Green Slate. The vicar wrote to us with his questions:

'Having studied the proposal carefully, I have two comments to make, bearing in mind the diocesan rules which I have to enforce:

'1. Do you consider the memorial to be straight sided?

'2. Is the (admittedly handsome) Tudor Rose a 'small' flower? My inexpert measurement makes it about 13% of the above-ground height of the stone.'

We were able to reassure the vicar about the 'straight sides' by sending him an example of a memorial in the same diocese of a similar shape, also by saying

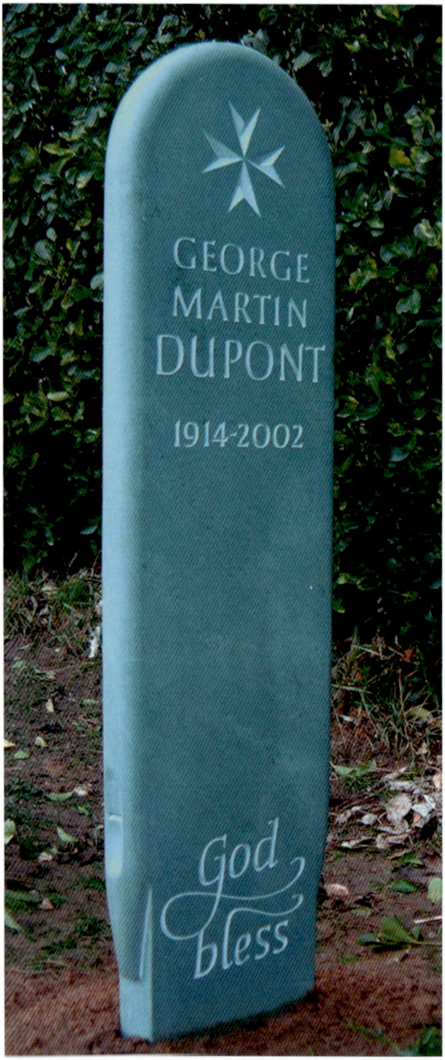

Teucer Wilson

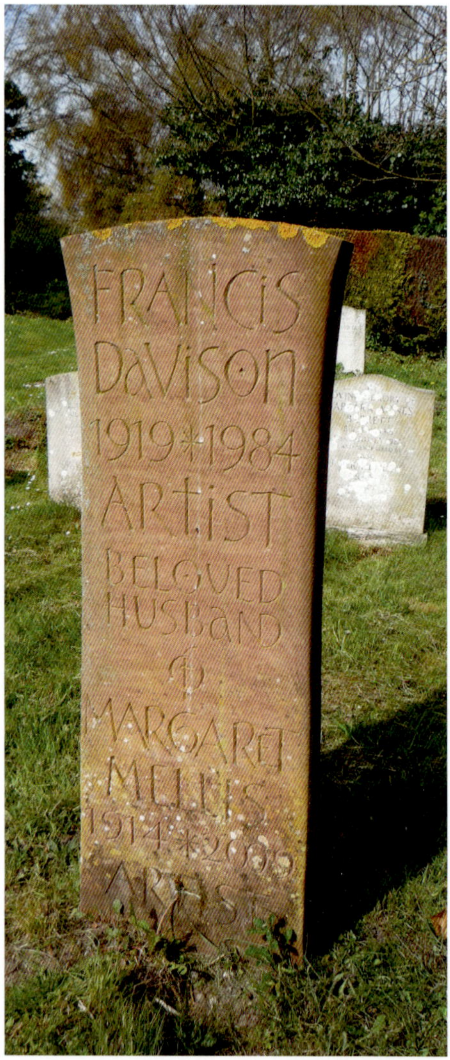

Jamie Sergeant

that we were sure that the Tudor Rose could be considered a small flower. We have a large number of headstones in churchyards throughout this diocese, many of which have flowers of a similar size, if not larger, and we have never had any objections raised about the size of the carving.'

Following our reassurance, permission was granted.

Headstone to George Martin Dupont

Miss Dupont told us she would like the headstone for her father to be made with 'mellowed and textured Cumberland Green Slate and some sort of design, if possible, with organ pipes and a St John's Maltese style cross. I would also like "God Bless" which our family uses as a goodbye phrase.'

Wonderfully, the incumbent gave permission for this memorial within a fortnight of receiving the application forms.

Headstone to Francis Davidson

Margaret Mellis wanted the headstone to her husband to be 'as tall as possible' and for the material to be the pinkish coloured St Bees Sandstone from Cumbria. The diocesan regulations stipulated a maximum height of 122cm (48 ins), so the height complied with the rules and there was no problem with permission. The headstone looks particularly tall in this photograph (and on p.44), with the relatively modern stones surrounding it being the more usual 75cm (30 ins) in height. As so often in our churchyards, there are several old stones nearer the church which are 160 cms (63ins) or more. It is important in these cases to look at the churchyard as a whole.

Headstone to Livi McKie

(see page 59)

It took several months to gain permission for this memorial. After asking Livi's mother if we could quote from her email (see article by The Reverend Peter Blee, p.58), I received her reply.

'As you know, the original design had Livi's full name only – Olivia Daisy Mitchell McKie – and although that wasn't wrong, it was only part of who she was. So when I opened Emily's second envelope and saw her name – and how sensitively Emily had placed it – the name we mostly called her, the name she mostly called herself, it was as if she was there, somehow; as if it was really her. So, if there are regulations that disallow nicknames or pet names on headstones they are very, very, *cruelly* wrong, because they don't allow the person to be there – *pace* your Introduction, they give the wrong answer to "who was she?".'

A HUMAN PRESENCE The Reverend Peter Blee

The expressive power of hand-written or in this case, stone cut lettering cannot be overstated. The creative process of making something beautiful and individual echoes, in its own condensed way, the uniqueness of the life of the individual being commemorated.

It does so in an affirming way, one which helps the bereaved in the painful process of acceptance. A memorial is arguably the last and most lasting expression of love towards the individual and with that comes an emotionally important sense of finality about the loss which can be difficult to handle. It is important to get it right and to be able to live with that final and lasting act of expression and commemoration. A memorial which has been beautifully hand-crafted has a 'soul', a life. It is seen in different ways and has different meanings at different times. It has an element of human responsiveness, a presence. This is partly a result of the creativity and skill of the craftsperson and also of the choices made by the bereaved in discussion with him/her which result in something deeply personal as well as being of artistic merit and beauty. When a memorial has been successfully created in this way there is sometimes a moment of recognition by the family, a moment when the memorial almost mediates the life of the person commemorated. It is as if the individual is literally in some way being 're-presented' to them in their loss, affirming the lasting meaning of that person's life and the things which are eternal and true for all time. One mother wrote: '...actually I knew the moment I took your new design out of the envelope that it was right. It was almost like a shock of recognition...'. Others experience it when the stone is put in place.

Also inherent in commissioning a hand-made memorial is the element of participating in tradition and continuity, a sharing in the human experience of loss and the manner in which it has been expressed through the centuries. It is a comfort to the bereaved to know that an artistic legacy has been left for others to enjoy.

A memorial forms the focus, at visits to the grave, for repeated acts of remembrance which punctuate the experience of bereavement. As such it has the potential to play an important role in that complex and agonising process. Yet a combination of not knowing how to handle the emotive significance of a memorial, lack of information about how to create one, what they can be like, and a lack of confidence about how and what to express, leads many people to opt for something 'safe' and uninvolved, something rather perfunctory and often machine-made. It might provide the necessary information, it might include words of meaning but it doesn't work in the more beneficial and dynamic way described above. Addressing this point of decision-making and informing people about the different kinds of memorials that can be created and the options available will make the greatest difference to the future of memorial art.

Emily Hoffnung

There are, of course, certain regulations or guidelines drawn up by the Chancellor of each Diocese for the sake of ensuring a certain degree of appropriateness, and these are to be welcomed. Certainly the appearance of the memorial should be in keeping with its setting, and the stone it is made from should relate to that of its environment. But there must also be scope for creativity and the more good examples that can be commissioned the more likely the regulations are to be adapted and modified accordingly.

This exhibition opens people's minds to the possibilities for memorials and encourages them to be more imaginative and expressive, and to realise the important opportunity which the commissioning of a memorial represents. It also promotes the work of those designer-craftsmen who have been given the special of gifts of working with stone. It is a contribution to the cultural and artistic tradition and identity of this country.

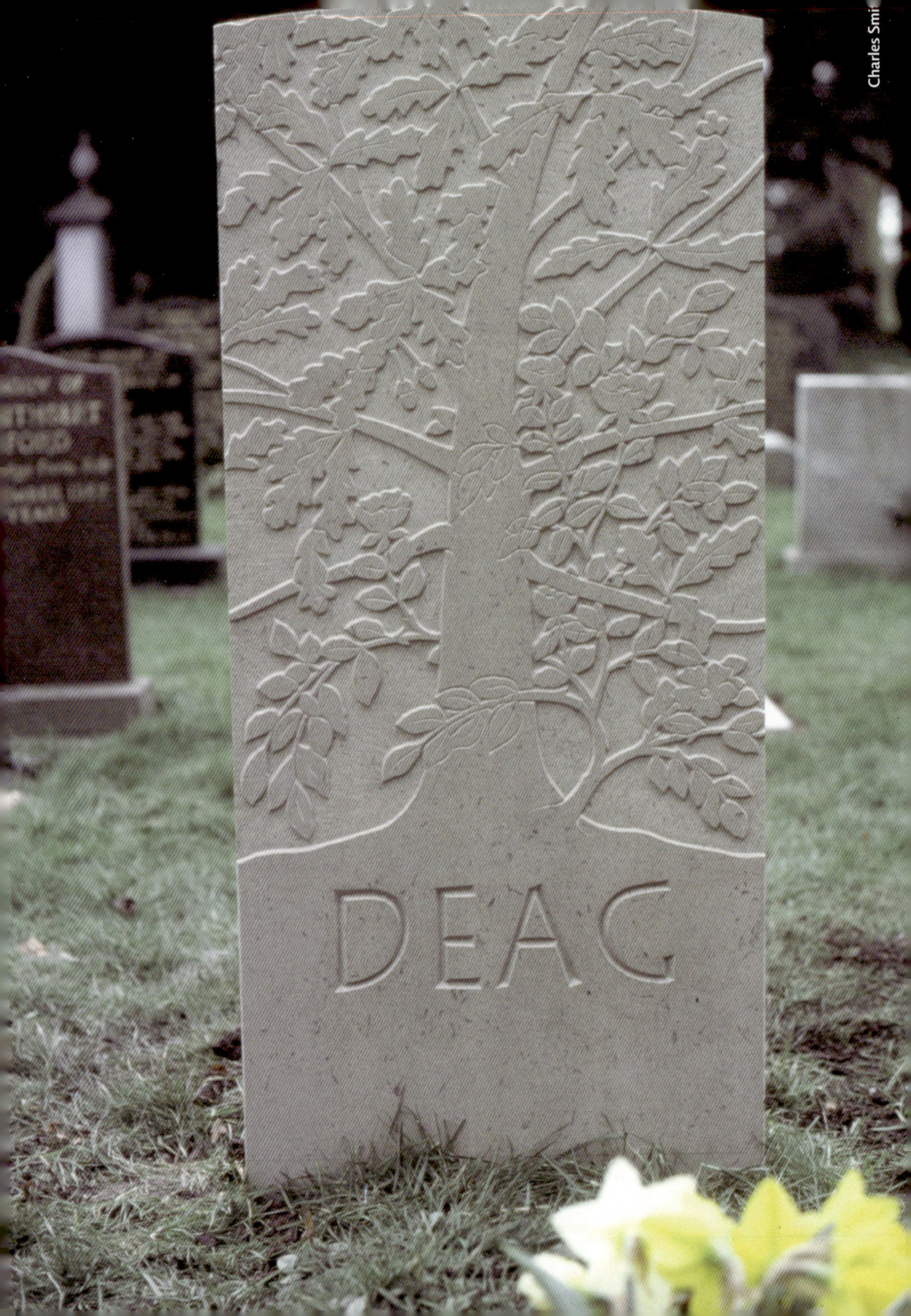

Charles Smi

SOME POINTS OF VIEW

I came to monumental carving by way of wood engraving and a concern with lettering and typography and the whole business of communication both by image and by 'visible words'. But love of the English landscape has also played its part. Geology has shaped the land itself, determining soils and vegetation and the materials of vernacular building, the variety of which so enriches the countryside. Among the special satisfactions of memorial work are those of continuing a traditional craft and making things as it were out of the bones of England to become a further part of the pattern.

The late Michael Renton, Lettercarver

Sometime lately I was in Burnsall on the River Wharfe (a very beautiful area). Eric Gill put a superb Portland Stone cross memorial in the churchyard in the 1930s and the design still looks modern today. But today he could not do it. He would need a faculty for the cross and it would fail on dimensions.

I have written elsewhere: 'Contemporary carvers are taking the opportunity of working not only the face but also the back, sides and top of the stone. Sooner or later it will be felt that this formula has been fully exploited. The sculptors of the future will have to have more to go at. They will have to have more scope if commemorative art is to really survive, and 'live'.'

Charles Smith, Lettercarver

I am concerned by the following phrase: 'A simple headstone. Its face must be flat and not significantly curved, rebated or recessed.' There is a fine and wonderful tradition of bold carving and strong masonry on old memorials. I think it would be very sad and a move in the wrong direction to lose this part of our wonderful churchyard heritage. We are heading towards everything being flat and uniform. I know uniform can sound positive in some ways as it is safe, but just take a minute to look at the older stones around us and I am sure you'll agree some of the nicest are anything but uniform. As a designer, I hope we can maintain a bit of freedom here rather than instil fear in those whose responsibility it is to grant permission.

Teucer Wilson, Lettercarver

I believe the fear of individual freedom is still as great, if not greater, today than it was in the sixteenth century, and that it is a fear which pervades every part of society: it is by no means limited to church authorities.

The fear of another's freedom runs deep in all of us, for it may pose a threat to our security. As long as I am in control, in charge, all is well. I am secure, therefore I am. But when others start threatening my security, then I must bring them under control. In spirituality there is a need of constant vigilance lest we become, unconsciously, controllers of others.

Gerard W Hughes, Jesuit priest and author of *God of Surprises*.
Excerpt from an article 'Free to Find our Deepest Desire', *The Tablet*, June 2000

It is immensely encouraging for a letter-cutter occasionally to be able to make something quite novel. There is room for all sorts and styles of stone, but it is worth remembering that the old stones which we think of as archetypal and ageless, were fresh and original in their day. Added to which, most inscriptions were probably painted, and not necessarily in subdued colours. Tastefulness is generally thought of as a virtue, but it can, it we don't watch it, become a negative one.

Nicholas Sloan, Lettercarver

(Likewise) the Church of England's ministry to the bereaved is sometimes undermined by churchyard regulations. A church for all cannot be cavalier about rules, but it must always be open to the more imaginative directions of the Holy Spirit.

The Rt Revd Nigel McCulloch, Bishop of Manchester. Excerpt from his article: 'A Church for all must sometimes bend the rules' (from the 'Credo' series, *The Times*, June 2000)

It has been suggested that the commissioning of a memorial 'can be part of the healing process'. The implication that the maker of memorials might be exercising a genuine ministry to the bereaved is inspired and inspiring, though the idea may not be at once familiar to everyone. The business of memorials is potentially a touchstone of many things: of ideas about death, obviously, but also of the whole ethos of making – of consumer attitudes and questions of supply and demand; of the place of art in belief and daily life; of spiritual priorities, our understanding of what constitutes humanity, and of the sacramental nature of things. Commissioning a memorial may seem a very personal and private affair but it is usually also a public act; the work will normally outlast several generations, if not centuries, becoming a historical document and witness to a culture. Pre-eminently, it is the sort of artefact from which people of the future will judge the quality of life and thought which produced it.

The late Michael Renton (1934–2001) wood engraver, book designer, calligrapher, lettercutter and carver. Michael designed and carved the woodblock for the letterheads of Memorials by Artists and The Memorial Arts Charity. He lived in Sussex for thirty years, moving to Winchester in 1994 as he was much involved in the design of lettering for Winchester Cathedral. Like Eric Gill before him, he designed his own headstone (opposite).

Michael Renton

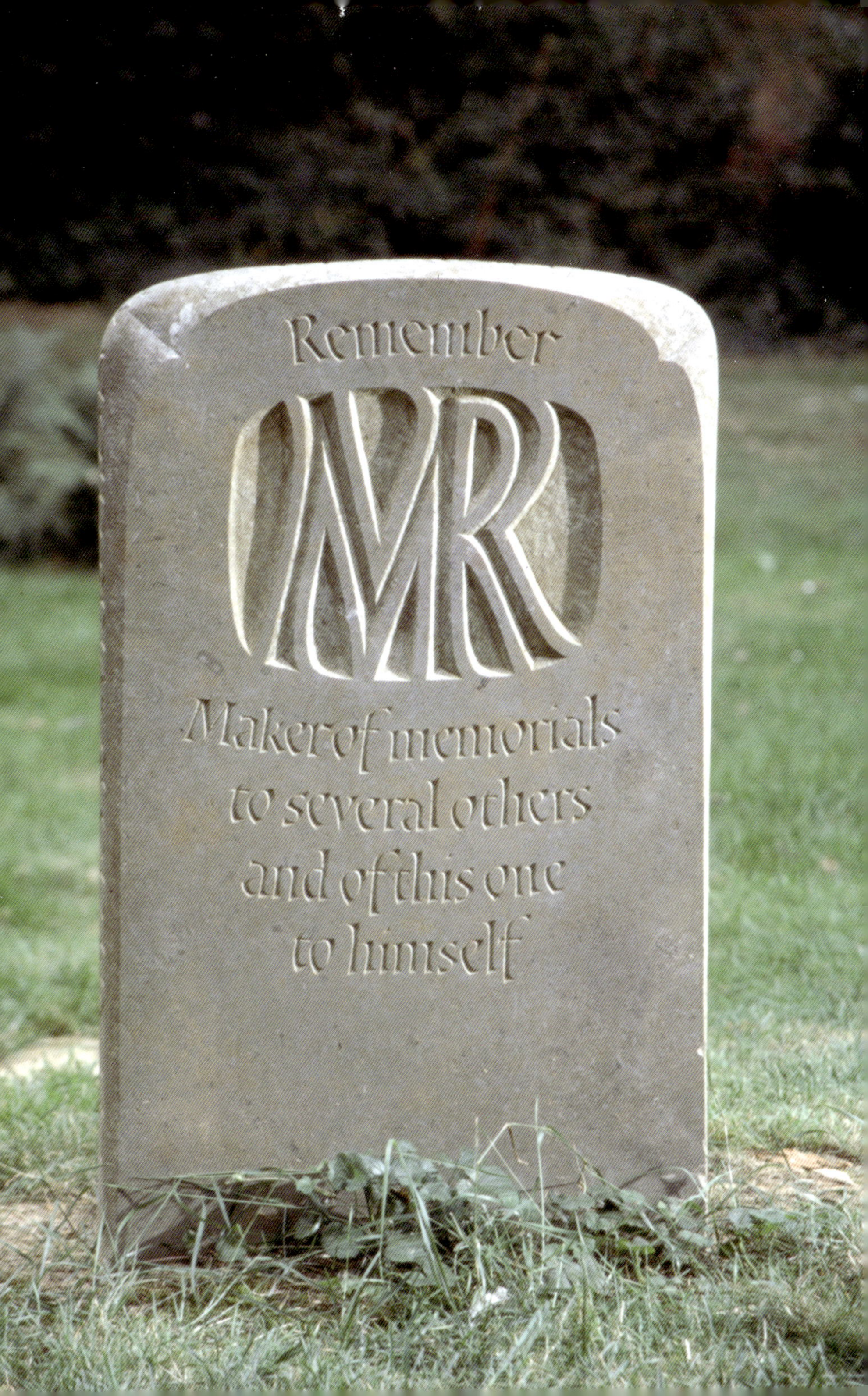

THE Memorial Arts CHARITY

Publications

Memorials by Artists
Fully revised fourth edition of this practical guide, illustrated in colour throughout.
£10 + £2 p&p

Memorials by Artists for Young People, Children and Babies
Over 70 full colour illustrations and several helpul articles.
£15 + £2·50 p&p

Art & Memory: New Perspectives on Memorial Art
The fully illustrated catalogue of the launch of The Art & Memory Collection (2009) at West Dean Gardens.
£5 + £1·50 p&p

DVD: a film by Jeremy Brettingham on the work of The Memorial Arts Charity (interviews with several lettercarvers, two apprentices, Harriet Frazer & Christine Oestreicher).
16 minutes.
£5 + £1·50 p&p

DVD: a film by Charlotte Trench on the Touch Workshops with blind and visually impaired children, featuring the children and tutors Kevin Carey (Chair of the RNIB) and Sally Booth.
£10 inc p&p

The Memorial Arts Charity
Snape Priory, Snape
Suffolk IP17 1SA
(01728) 688393
www.memorialartscharity.org.uk
Registered Charity no.1071427

Memorials by Artists
Snape Priory, Snape
Suffolk IP17 1SA
(01728) 688934
www.memorialsbyartists.co.uk
Company Registered in England no.3680450

Acknowledgements

The Chairman & Trustees of The Memorial Arts Charity; The Churches Conservation Trust; Amberley Parochial Church Council; Horsham District Council; Sussex Community Council Grassroots Programme; H D Tribe Limited; The Monumental Company Limited; Mr Peter Legge; Mr & Mrs David Lock; Mrs Jacqueline Agar; Mrs Gwen Hall; Hennings Wine Merchants; Chichester Diocesan Advisory Committee

Credits

We would like to thank all the artists who have made works for the Art & Memory Collection, all of whom have donated a good deal of their time. Also our grateful thanks to Janet Aidin and all the others involved in the Art & Memory North Stoke exhibition, too many to name individually, for their unstinting help and advice; and to all the artists and authors whose help has made this catalogue possible.

Exhibition designer, Janet Harker

Photographs by the individual artists; Phil Baines & Kate Lyons; Ellen Cheshire; Dee Harris Photography; Oliver Riviere; Anthea Sieveking; p.54: top left from Betty Wilshire & Doreen Hunter, *Understanding Scottish Graveyards*, Canongate 1977

Designed by Phil Baines
& Kate Lyons
Printed by Ripping Image